THE SENTIENT PATHWAY

I0081678

GLOBAL
PUBLISHING
G R O U P

Global Publishing Group
Australia • New Zealand • Singapore • America • London

THE SENTIENT PATHWAY

The #1 Guide to Developing Your Intuition, Giving You Power, Clarity and Confidence

ENDORSED BY THE COLLEGE OF INTUITION

BEN & KIM SOWTER

"Intuition doesn't tell you what you want to hear; it tells you what you need to hear."
– Sonia Choquette

A catalogue record for this book is available from the National Library of Australia

Published by Global Publishing Group
PO Box 517 Mt Evelyn, Victoria 3796 Australia
Email info@GlobalPublishingGroup.com.au

For further information about orders:
Phone: +61 3 9739 4686 or Fax +61 3 8648 6871

*Dedicated to those who have inspired
and assisted us to make this book a reality.*

Kim's Acknowledgements

The Sentient Pathway could not have been made possible without the loving encouragement of my husband Ben. May we write, teach, love and challenge each other for many more lives to come.

To the physical teachers who have mentored my journey with their tireless humour, optimism and faith. I am eternally grateful; Carmel Bell, Carol Crawford, The Victorian Spiritualist Union, Pat, Drew Sinton (who showed me light and dark exist as one), Master Mikhail.

I would love to thank my guides who work with me constantly, Anaterrea, Silver Moon, White Feather, Prophet Seer, and those who dropped in. May peace be with you.

To my loving mother Margaret Platzer, my first teacher and guiding force with the world of spirit. Your lack of fear with the unknown and faith in a higher power has given me the strength to keep going in moments of doubt.

To my father Alfred Platzer, you have been the most challenging teacher of all. I thank you for letting me learn what it truly means to let go and release.

To Lawrence Ellyard for giving an enthusiastic yes, and the team of International Institute for Complimentary Therapies (IICT) for giving all of us who dare to dream the means of making our work a little easier.

To the team of Global Publishing, thank you for the ideas, endless support and enthusiasm.

Ben's Acknowledgements

It has been an absolute joy, honour, and life achievement to have co-authored this book. As this book has been inspired by my journey, many people who have inspired me and contributed to my learning and understanding of *The Sentient Pathway* have ultimately helped make this book a reality.

Thank you to my sister, Nicole, who provided the catalyst audio CD that initiated my journey of self-discovery. Thank you to my Mother – Lyn, Father – Steven and Brother - Heath for giving me the environment for growth and learning that has formed into the person I am.

My wife Kim Sowter is an amazing, loving and compassionate woman, with her strong connection to the spirit realm and I thank her with all my heart for inspiring, assisting and supporting me on countless occasions over the years we have been together.

Thank you to those not in the physical – my spirit team that were there all those years even when I didn't know it.

To my teachers, Carmel Bell and Carol Crawford-Kerr; Carmel, you are an inspiring person who taught me how to heal and manage my energetic body and Carol, how to trust my ability to communicate to the spirit world.

To the Dalai Lama; your selfless journey of sharing the middle way with the world; you changed my world and opened my heart.

Thank you to the inspirational founders of modern sound healing and vocal toning such as, Jonathan Goldman who founded the modern-day method of sound healing and created astounding recordings, Tom Kenyon who's vocal range and technique encouraged me to explore my abilities, David Hykes for the amazing Harmonic Choir, Steven Halpern for your recordings, as well as many more sonic masters.

FREE BONUS AUDIO DOWNLOAD

To further enhance your intuitive development, we have created a number of unique audio recordings that are designed to complement the exercises in this book.

These audio recordings use powerful sound frequencies to clear the mind and shift your consciousness to a higher vibratory state of intuition.

For more information about the power of sound frequencies, be sure to read the BONUS chapter – Voice of the Soul.

Get

INSTANT ACCESS TO YOUR FREE BONUS AUDIO DOWNLOAD

by going to

www.thesentientpathway.com/freebonusdownload

Contents

Foreword

It is a pleasure to write a few introductory words to this book on Intuition, *The Sentient Pathway* by Kim and Ben Sowter.

Intuition is often misunderstood, referred to as an instinct to be relied on for survival. It is so much more. Today, quantum science has been able to verify that we receive a wealth of information from our environment, so much in fact that it has a bearing on our thoughts and can affect our physical body. Intuition is the gateway to understanding our personal relationship with ourselves, our tribe and the world we live in.

Well done to Kim and Ben who have made sense of a subject that can be filled with complexities and misunderstanding. The book breaks down the relationship we commonly have with our daily intuitive sense. Taking the reader on a journey of discovering as to why their insights, senses and feelings can often lead to the right path despite all the intellectual knowledge that tells us otherwise.

I have been listening to my intuition for years which has let me to understand that this sense is an important tool for accessing inner wisdom. Alerting us to so many things that the conscious mind cannot. The ability to sense when we need help before it happens or to know the direction we need to take to find our answers are all based on the connection to our intuition.

Kim and Ben have weaved scientific facts with years of practical experience, working in the field of intuition for health, mindset, soul connection and spirituality. With this experience, they have been able to provide an in depth look at all aspects of intuition.

I understand why Kim and Ben have asked me to write the foreword. It is a book that I encourage to anyone who is interested in exploring the mind–body relationship to dip into the pages of *The Sentient Pathway*. The practical techniques can be applied daily to any aspect of life. Work through the chapters to unleash the power of self-trust. Do this and it won't be long before the belief that you can heal and create whatever you choose in this lifetime becomes a reality.

The answers we want already exist within, coded into our very being. It is just a matter of knowing how to tap into this infinite source. *The Sentient Pathway* is the book that will provide the tools for the journey of life.

Lawrence Ellyard

Founder / CEO the International Institute

for Complementary Therapists

www.iict.com.au

Kim's Introduction

Everything is written in the stars, it's just a matter of getting it on paper.

For many years I had been told there is a book that has been written. "Spirit said it is finished." This had been said many times by various psychics and channels. I always laughed, shaking my head because many, many notes had been written but this had not created a book, until now.

All of us were born open to utilising our inner senses for communicating with each other in the physical and the spiritual realms, and to access the answers we need in life from our own higher consciousness. I chose to remember this, but many did not and here we have a conundrum. The ability to communicate with higher intelligence – to see, feel the past, present and future, to experience phenomena that is not understood by science. We either choose to believe or not and unfortunately the seeming majority have made it very difficult to accept that each of us has an innate ability to connect with the 'truth of all that is'. Enforcing the view that those who openly discuss their experiences or views are unstable, 'nutty' or just laughed at and dismissed, nor enticed from producing any validation.

With such varied views towards the 'paranormal', most of my life has consisted of a love-hate relationship with my own ability. I chose to develop clairvoyance and spirit communication for the purpose of understanding myself. What I didn't anticipate was going on to assist others to receive guidance and help to remember their own connections.

I have been ridiculed and dismissed by those who simply give their will to the mass opinion of disbelief. All the while, I have envied their ignorance, thinking how much easier it would be to live a life of limited perception. Now, I can see there is a change in the air, an awakening and sharing of knowledge that goes beyond the physical happenings of day to day routine. People are waking up and beginning to remember life beyond the physical.

With life experience and a wonderful collaboration between myself, Ben and those who placed trust in us to navigate the meaning behind, sensory perception, we give you *The Sentient Pathway*.

Ben's Introduction

I welcome and congratulate you for embarking on your journey of self-discovery. The very fact you are reading this book is evidence your intuition is guiding you on *The Sentient Pathway*. This is a journey that not everyone will take, let alone be ready to walk it. This pathway is about truly understanding all aspects of who you are, many aspects of which others will never see. It is a journey of knowing thyself, as well as being guided to heal and change parts of your being along the way. It is a constantly evolving journey that will never take a backward step.

It was my journey that inspired me to co-author this book, sharing the culmination of 20 or more years of my life experiences and learning. There seems to have been a recent shift in our collective consciousness which now allows us to recognise the innate enlightened intuition ability we have is something that is very real and tangible. There probably has never been a more important time for this shift, as our lives seem to get more complex and busy, with less face-to-face interaction that ever before. It is important and timely for us to reconnect to ourselves and understand our origin, which in time will help in the reconnection of all of us, as we are all one and the same.

Our intuition is the ability with which we access the information of our soul's purpose, our journey in this life. It guides us through our life, helping us to understand what choice needs to be made and why. Through this journey of reconnecting to our intuition, we learn to trust that part of ourselves that is not physical or visible, but still the very essence of who we are; our soul essence. It is this journey of integrating our spiritual selves with the physical, *The Sentient Pathway*, that leads us to growth and enlightenment as a being.

How To Use This Book

The Sentient Pathway is an introductory guide for anyone who is embarking on a journey of self-exploration towards a state of heightened awareness through their innate intuition. It also includes content that will suit readers with some experience in using intuition. It is suggested that after the initial reading, this book can become a great source of encouragement as the reader progresses further along their Sentient Pathway.

Both authors are aware that individuals will have their own experiences, thoughts and beliefs prior to reading this book. At no point is there any attempt to ridicule or dismiss religious beliefs or practice. Instead, this book transcends man-made religious belief, empowering the individual to connect to their higher consciousness and allowing for co-creation with the divine source of creation.

With the many practical exercises included, the journey that the book takes the reader on is best approached with an open mind and a willingness to explore the deeper facets of human sensitivity. This may include acknowledging and identifying hidden aspects of the self that need to be transformed into a healthier and more balanced aspect. Each technique may be practiced once or several times, depending on the needs of the individual to achieve the desired result.

The bonus chapter – Voice of The Soul – contains information and powerful techniques on how to use sound frequencies to clear the conscious mind and raise the consciousness to the level of intuition, both of which are vital aspects of intuition development. Be sure to download the bonus free audio recordings as mentioned in the free bonus download page, as these tracks with their powerful sound frequencies are designed to complement the written exercises in the book.

The Sentient Pathway has been written from personal experience. As such, it was difficult not to write from a personal point of view, therefore we have included the author's name at the beginning of each chapter.

The book makes reference to the physical and mental changes that can occur when undertaking intuitive development. If the results lead to physical discomfort beyond 'normal', then we advise seeking medical attention. We do not recommend or promote going against any current medical advice nor believe that intuitive development is a replacement for current medical assistance.

Both authors Kim and Ben strongly disagree with the use of drugs in any form to enhance intuitive or mystical experiences. Neither author has ever relied on drugs as an enhancement or means of receiving a direct, clear connection to intuition or spiritual beings.

The Sentient Pathway is a guide to living a wonderful life by utilising the innate sensory system to obtain guidance, answers and a deep connection that will enforce the union of body, mind and soul.

Definition

Sentient Being

1 – An individual who absorbs sensory stimulus from the environment and personal interactions.

2 – To live by sensory perception means to go with the flow of life; eliminating opposition or force.

CHAPTER 1

Getting Started

CHAPTER 1

Getting Started

Written by Kim

You are already intuitive; allowing the mind to be conscious of this fact is where the development begins. The ego often overrides any feeling, spark of inspiration or creative idea by using self-talk disguised as an intellectual thought to alter what intuition is trying to say.

You may be driving when a strong feeling to turn left is overshadowed by the intellect. Failing to listen to feeling, you turn right and head towards a traffic pile up. Frustrated, you end up sitting in traffic thinking "If I had gone left, I could have avoided this. Why didn't I listen?" You didn't listen because you failed to trust what your inner GPS was telling you.

Developing intuition can often seem like a constant battle between intellect and inner sensing. The ego holds on, fighting to be heard out of fear of losing control from the world that we have become accustomed to living in. All that is currently known to be true, including what has taught by family, teachers and social conformity, the ego holds. Unravelling all that is held tests our own self-trust, pushing the boundaries of limitation to unleash the inner force of knowledge and wisdom.

The fear of what it means to let go of all we hold and live a life of trust prevents many from obtaining an intuitive link, and living a life of grace co-created with divine will. Help yourself by letting go of control, and practice living with the flow of life – this includes listening to the inner senses, the pull, the knowing and hearing the voice of guidance.

Letting go does not mean you have no control at all, in fact, it gives more credit to the choices and pathway that you want to take without all the rubbish that can get in the way when we try to control or manipulate outcomes.

Whenever we hold group training, we watch participants undertake techniques to assist with letting go of the ego. We can observe the ones who find it difficult, mainly because they begin to show emotion, either looking teary, flushed or just plain uncomfortable. That's okay because they probably didn't realise how much their head was ruling everything in life.

As soon as the awareness of ego is present, we can see just how much our thoughts and control override the inner connection. It is amazing to see how people respond to this insight, some cry, other shift body language from closed to open and the rest will ask, "How do I let go?" Now we let the real development begin.

Before delving into intuitive techniques and all the amazing benefits that it brings, we have outlined three crucial areas to be discussed – trust, choice and what happens when there is no apparent intuitive insight.

Trust

High on its perch the bird watched the world go by, wondering what it would be like to fly into the sky. The door unlocked, the bird was offered the chance to explore.

"If I leave the cage what will be waiting for me? I do not want to be in this cage, but I know how it comforts me. I know no different, so I think I will stay. Maybe one day I will change."

We all want the courage to leave the cage and fly into the sky, but it takes trust to really let go and allow the freedom of living to flow. When we lack self-trust, it becomes difficult to make decisions and leads to second guessing ourselves.

Trust creates the change needed to live the life we desire. If we do not trust ourselves to drive, then we would never get behind the steering wheel.

Just like the bird, our known experiences are comforting, they allow us to stay in our present circumstances even if we do not like them. The ego tells us that this is the best place to be while courage keeps it all in place. The illusion is that we believe life is meant to be this way.

Becoming in tune with intuition will naturally play on the relationship that you have with trust. Questioning every feeling, thought or happening. Is it my mind or is it intuition? This is the outcome of previous conditioning.

Intuition is not emotionally driven so be alert of the thoughts that surface, because if emotions are attached then it is more than likely a by-product of past teachings manifesting as intuition. Emotions can create fear which will then cause trust issues.

The story of the bird highlights the power that emotions have on our thoughts and inability to trust ourselves. The bird sees the cage as a link to feeling safe. When the door is opened the bird feels uneasy. Taking a step towards freedom the bird's held beliefs surface – "Don't do that. You don't know what's out there. You may be hurt or never come back" – these feelings are so overwhelming that the bird is forced by fear to remain in the comfort it has become used to.

As the bird demonstrated, our fears become reality when we fail to listen within. Luckily, human beings are wonderful at adapting to surroundings and changing their minds within a second.

Trust is often learned by listening to others, we become trusting because a link to feeling safe is established. When life is going well we trust that all is okay and often we attribute this to something outside ourselves whether that is God, the universe or a parent or teacher but when the trust is no longer there, we are let down and our mind holds onto the memory, stored away to be used as a validation of why we can't change.

The reality is we experience trust from within. To be able to comprehend that a decision is based on your ability to know what is best for you is an example of self-trust. Intuition and trust are intertwined, both are needed to receive the full power of what is possible.

Tips for Trusting Intuition

- Intuition does not have emotional attachment

- Trust is intertwined with intuition and cannot be separated

- Fears become reality when we fail to listen to the truth within

- Thoughts and emotions may be linked to the unconscious giving a false sense of security and preventing what may be a positive decision

The Power of Choice

The journey of intuition begins with the connection we have to ourselves along with the choices that are made. To pursue intuition is a choice based on the need of opening the mind to greater self-awareness.

The choices we make result in a conscious decision to alter life circumstances. The results are made from the freedom to choose how we react, live and interact within the world. Knowing we have a choice will lead to greater joy and happiness. Remaining asleep, unconscious of the ability to evolve our way of being will keep us enslaved to current limitations.

Life has a wonderful way of honouring choices by manifesting the circumstances that will reinforce what we believe to be true. If we believe deep down that our life is to be a continual burden of work, financial stress and limited joy, then it will be. Alter this core belief to be in line with how you want to feel, and the perception of the world and circumstances will transform with you.

Developing intuition will unleash the core beliefs, pushing the boundaries of free thinking with limited vision. Emotions, physical symptoms, thoughts and dreams can reveal the pain of past hurts. Do not let this awareness stop you from continuing with development.

There will be a logical processing of regret for past actions undertaken by you and others. Everyone has a regret of some degree, but do not hold onto this, let it go. Clear the burden of what should have been and focus on all the freedom that is with you now.

Ego will lead us to think that we have no choice, our life is locked in by responsibilities. The simple truth is, we all have the ability to choose how we think, feel and act. We have a choice to give up, be unhappy and never do anything different or we can ask for help, seek guidance and free the mind from its prison.

Tips for Making Choices

- The deeper the connection to ourselves the more conscious our ability to choose

- Core beliefs create life circumstances

- Choices we make result in a conscious decision to alter current positioning

When Intuition Disappears

We have discussed the relationship of trust and choice in establishing a conscious link with intuition. In both cases there is a common theme; past events bring emotions to the surface that create thoughts of doubt and fear.

Human beings were made with the ability to express emotions – it is what enables us to physically demonstrate compassion. Life would be boring if we did not have emotions. There will be times when our emotions may become overwhelming, causing inspiration to fade and our intuition to seem like it has disappeared.

There is good news; intuition never leaves, it can't, it is part of who we are. When the emotions become heightened, it's hard to think clearly, and our intuitive ability fails to be recognised. A little bit like a radio that cannot find a clear station because of all the static interfering with the waves of frequency.

The first thing to remember is, don't beat yourself up about not receiving any insights. It may just be that part of you wants to do nothing at all, but we tell ourselves there needs to be an excuse to rest.

We see this a lot where individuals have been conditioned to give or be of service to humanity. Maybe your parents instilled the belief of 'it is better to give than to receive'. It is wonderful to give, but it is also important to receive.

Many intuitives often choose a career which focuses on being of service, such as healing, health, customer service, etc. If the individual is constantly giving out and not receiving an imbalance causes overload. You may be familiar with the term 'burnt out'. Again, we can use the radio as an example; when there is a surge of electrical current to the radio, the device blows a fuse. Fortunately, unlike the radio human beings have a consciousness that can choose to let go and self-nurture or continue until the mind, body and soul are completely incapable of going on.

It doesn't help that our modern lifestyle consists of so many demands that we fail to take note of how we are travelling on a personal level. The choice to change course and stop for a while seems obvious, but often we ignore it. Eventually, ill health, excess fatigue, physical pain or changes to thought processes indicating stress bring an enforced change.

What do we do? Invoke the mind to become aware of when life is becoming too much of a struggle. Let go and do nothing. It is easy to take time each day for yourself, remember it is only old conditioned patterns of, 'I should', 'I have to', that prevent self-nurturing.

It may be that you find yourself with the challenge of a stressful situation. Before the emotions kick in and cloud any judgement, stop, take a break, re-centre yourself by breathing deeply and just relax.

A friend of ours, Carmen, has discovered the ability to let go.

Carmen held a high-pressure job as a real estate agent. Part of her role was to show beautiful properties to high-end clients. Carmen's reputation within the industry was well known; she prided herself on being well organised and mentally attuned to her clients, attributes that provided much success. So, when she lost the only set of keys to a property Carmen immediately thought of how her reputation would become tainted.

The poor woman frantically searched the home, in the garden and then finally her car. Then a thought crossed her mind that maybe they had dropped out of her bag when she had to stop for petrol. The idea of someone picking them up caused overwhelming anxiety. You see, the keys were not only the one set, but they had the address listed on the key ring.

Carmen's mind let that little voice of regret take over, telling her how stupid it was not to have a second set and how remiss to have lost them in the first place. Her mind told her that this was such a stupid mistake, something a rookie would make, not an established realtor.

Finally, she got into her car and drove to the service station. Realising the keys were not there she just sat in the car and did nothing. Two hours went by, and she honestly can't remember what happened because the time just flew, but she was calm enough to reach down the side of her seat. Her finger was brushing onto a bit of metal. Carman looked down and could just make out what looked like the cut edge of a key. Pushing the seat as far back as she could, she took out her nail file, got out the car and pulled up the set of keys. Sometimes it pays just to let go, let be and wait.

Humans are delicate, sensitive beings that require nurturing. We do not have to be exposed to our drama to feel the emotions. The nightly news or social media can often be a source for receiving too much devastation which impacts on our well-being. Choose to listen to positive music, spend time in nature, have a warm bath, read a good book, whatever it is for you that allows the mind and body to be still. In the moments of stillness, we find our answers.

Tips for Reconnecting to Intuition

- Take time out each day to do nothing

- When self-doubt kicks in, let go, let be and wait

- Connecting with nature will anchor your mind, body and soul back to the present moment

- Self-nurturing is a necessity not a luxury

CHAPTER 2

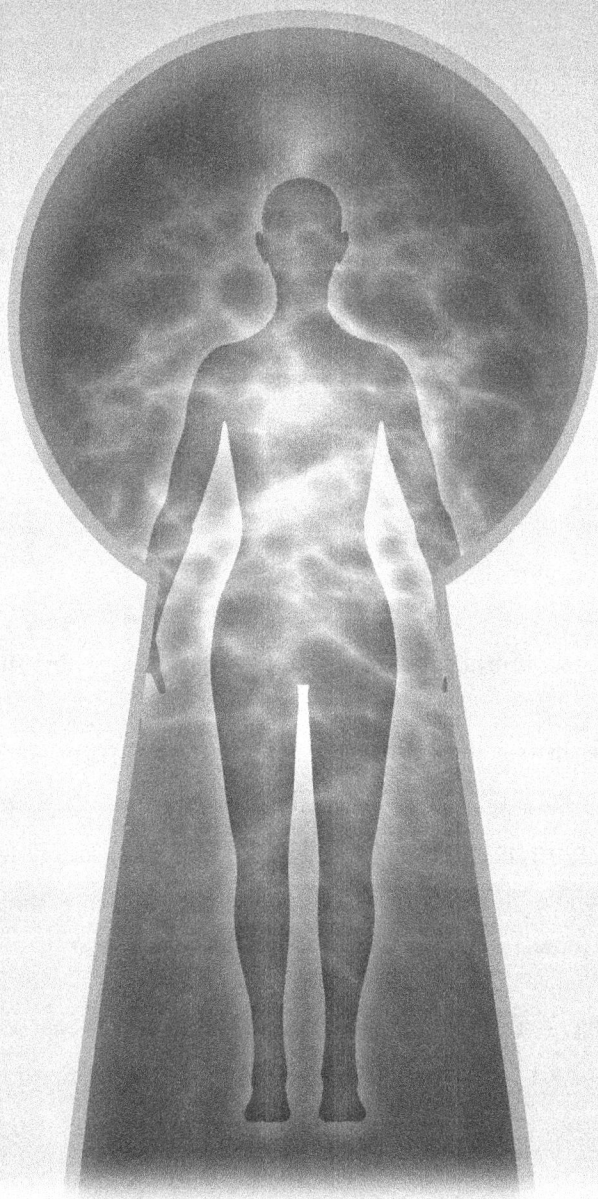

What is Intuition?

CHAPTER 2

What is Intuition?

Written by Kim

It appears everyone has a view on what intuition is. Some believe it to be a connection to the spiritual realm, or basic instinctual responses to events or past experiences held by the subconscious which surface when faced with a life choice. Intuition is all of this and much more, making this one of the most confusing and underutilised of human capabilities.

We have simply defined intuition as:

Inner wisdom, inner learning, inner sensing = Intuition

As simplistic as the definition sounds, the path of intuitive development can be an overwhelming journey into self-exploration. Beginning with attempting to understand how the mind functions, what and where do the thoughts come from, before then moving into the body's physical reactions. Why do I feel this way?

Before long, self-analysis leads to a cycle of moods, emotions, thoughts and frustrations that prevent further development or a path towards seeming loneliness. Others will not understand what you are going through, instead they see someone pulling apart every aspect of life, overanalysing, which leads to new burdens and fatigue. In the end, what has it achieved?

Human beings like to accumulate knowledge by understanding what makes something work. It is not in our intellectual nature, to simply accept. Rarely do we think about how breathing or blinking works, we know that the body will take care of this function with little effort or thought on our part. Do we believe we are separate from our body? Of course, not and what of the mind? We think all the time without effort, never assuming the mind is separate from our being. The confusion begins when we look beyond mind and body.

The soul is the essence of our being, the basis of identity. Unlike the mind and body, we question the existence of the soul.

The soul communicates through our heart as unconditional love and compassion. The heart remains as our human link to the soul and what we will work with to strengthen the connection with intuition.

Throughout this guide we will stretch the mind beyond its current limits, connect with the body and reunite the soul back to the conscious memory. The body, mind and soul are interlinked but to assist with the undertaking of your journey to intuition we have divided the sentient being into three aspects:

- The body, a vehicle to physically express our mind and determine our course
- The mind, used for logic, reason and intellectual knowledge
- The heart, the integration point for exchange centre for soul, body and mind

Intuition is the thread entwining the three aspects of self. When these aspects are in balance, a harmony resonates that is felt internally by the individual. The inner harmony resonates outward and may affect others who are near. Have you ever thought, "That person has a great energy?" When someone is in balance with their inner harmony the emotions, thoughts and feelings are clear and sequenced to create ideas.

Unfortunately, the Western world favours the intellectual mind over the ability to receive information through feeling or knowing. The result is the heart suffers, becoming laden with the burden of emotional blocks caused by too much rational thinking, which leads to worry while the body is pushed to keep working, stay functioning with minimal nurturing. With little focus for ourselves and lots of emphasis placed on external demands the natural flow of intuition becomes stifled. Basics instinct is no longer felt and nor is the subtle voice of guidance heard.

How do we keep going? The physical body requires nourishment to sustain optimal health. Food, exercise and water sustain the body enough to persevere. It is the mind that often pushes the body further, worrying about how we look or how far can we push the boundaries of physicality to see what we are capable of.

What happens to the heart when the mind and body are pressured? The heart takes the brunt of all the emotions that have resulted from thoughts, feelings and physical actions of the body. It is not by chance that we use such terms as, heartache or heartbroken when we feel sad. The heart is the centre for the emotions to be processed before the body expresses itself through tears or laughter.

The soul holds the key to why we were born and what we are here for. True passion, likes and dislikes beyond parental expectations, exist with the soul. It is often demonstrated throughout life as fine threads interwoven with everyday occurrences. For example, many others have viewed certain qualities you possess that are viewed as a calling. Perhaps throughout life you have been told that you would make a great teacher, nurse, artist or writer. The mind has only viewed the terms through limited vision. Your career interests open the door to a job in the financial world. The boss asks that you give numerous presentations to colleagues explaining the work that is normally undertaken. Enjoying this, the boss then pays for further development as a training facilitator. Before you know it the idea of teaching others seems amusing. The observations of others were correct – it was the mind that limited the opportunity by defining teaching as standing in front of a blackboard in a traditional schoolroom.

The soul and heart work closely by monitoring freedom of being. Simply put, are you receiving the experiences that the soul wants to have? Beyond the formed limitations placed by family and social conditioning?

Intuition is the thread that connects to the soul and our physical identity. When we feel pulled to go in a certain direction or receive insight such as a fortuitous dream, or have an idea that is wonderful and seemingly out of nowhere. It is intuition translating the language of the soul with human awareness.

Thankfully, many people are acknowledging there is more to life beyond the physical. However, the trials of modern day living have most of us relying on technology for quick fixes, resulting in dependence for finding answers outside of the self instead of reconnecting back to the inner self.

Taking away the dependence on devices will enforce reliance back to us. Either the rational mind will continue to allow the intellect to dominate or the inner self with prevail and we choose to go back to a natural state of living.

Learning to balance the mind, body and heart will encourage further awareness to the effects of thought, feeling and human interaction. Consciously the forms of intuition that weave the connection to create dreams, instincts, vision or knowing will provide understanding that this innate ability is not found with the intellect but rather through the bypassing of logic and rationality.

We will leave the example of just how intuition can weave between the mind, body and soul to provide the answers that logic may not understand.

One man's discovery demonstrates the importance of embracing intuition.

A man must find the answer to a problem. He reads all the books he can on the subject but does not find an answer.

Overworked and tired he falls asleep and dreams of a herd of cows being electrocuted. The cows, one by one jump away from the fence.

Waking up from the dream, he worked out a theory. The perception of an outcome changes depending on where you stand to watch an event.

The man was Einstein, the dream – the Special Theory of Relativity.

CHAPTER 3

Understanding Intuitive Forms

CHAPTER 3

Understanding Intuitive Forms

Written by Kim

Intuition is like a thread weaving through our body, mind and heart. Creating feeling, inspiring creativity and connecting back to the essence of our being, the soul.

Dependent on our state of being, intuition may be received in various ways, such as dreams that can predict future events or provide insight into current situations; a deep sense of knowing that may oppose rationality; or even a direct answer received as inner dialogue. Intuition is a constant connection that we have aligned with the three human aspects of body, mind and heart.

- Instinct – The physical body – Experienced as a physical feeling, fight or flight

- Inspired – The mind – Self-expression, dreams, artistic pursuits

- Enlightened – The heart – Integration of the soul with the mind and body. Having, knowledge, understanding, awareness and expression of compassion with all that exists.

Instinct – Body

Instinctual intuition is like receiving a yes/no question and answer. Good for basic awareness but lacking the detail to really place trust around the decision.

Common Forms of Instinct

- Feeling

- Gut instinct

- Hunch

Intuition is at best, a base line instinct referenced as the flight or fight response. Our ancestors relied on it for hunting by avoiding danger from predators. Keeping in tune with nature helped to prepare for immediate harm or an abundant harvest.

In today's world not much has changed, our instinct to survive kicks in strongly when danger is seemingly lurking nearby. Do we listen?

Think of a situation when you may have met someone for the first time, and that feeling of foreboding overshadowed the desire to reciprocate the polite, smiling handshake. Did the encounter have the hairs on the back of your neck stand up, a tingle down the spine and a queasy feeling in the stomach?

Maybe one, or all the physical sensations occurred. Your instinct is alerting you to something that the rational mind could not. What do you do? Walk away, continue the meeting only to find that there didn't seem to be any need to worry. They seemed nice.

The meeting is broken up by another person or they simply walk away. Thankfully, leaving you to breathe easier and letting the body go back a state of calmness.

The next day a friend calls you to say that they went on a date with the very person that made you feel uneasy. Immediately, the queasy sensation in the stomach comes back. Your friend tells you how this person tried to force themselves on them, but they managed to get away.

The above story may sound like an extreme case, however it did happen to one of our clients. She came to see us just to have her instincts validated and gain a better understanding of how to work with intuition.

Instinct does not have to reach the level of fear before it is acknowledged. People receive instinctual information from walking into a room. The sensations may be anything from joyful to sadness or just tension. The best example is when attending a house inspection. You don't know who was or is living on the property and they are never there when you walk into the building. So many clients have expressed how a home makes them 'feel' when they are looking for the right one to buy. It may have great features, but! The body is sensing that something is wrong however the mind has no rational explanation and therefore fear kicks in to create excuses of why not to buy the home.

For the novice of intuition development, going with feeling would be enough evidence to dismiss living in the home. The intuitive practitioner would know that once they moved in all the home needs is a good clean and house-welcoming to be rid of the residual energy.

The ability to sense the ambience of a room or feel empathic towards another human being is the basis for what makes us sentient beings. Relying on pure instinct alone may serve a survival purpose but it will not insight details of when, where or how. The sentient being has an appetite for learning about the self; this inspires relationships, career, family, ambition and a life that is full of hope and aspiration.

Inspired Intuition – Mind
When the logical mind is sleeping, inspiration awakens

If there is a solution to every problem, then inspired intuition is the key that unlocks the inner vault of answers. Be ready – unlike instinctual intuition which is relayed as a feeling of good or bad, yes or no, inspired intuition is an array of visual, sensory and even auditory pieces of information that require the individual to absorb their message without allowing the logical mindset of disbelief to take over.

Each one of us can relate to inspiration in its many forms but very few are aware just how the creative mind is a doorway for intuitive insight.

- Dreams
- Music
- Art, painting, drawing
- Writing
- Inspirational speaking
- Synchronicity

Even the most rational mind can relate to experiencing one or more of the above list. Unfortunately, most people fail to understand the relevance that this has within their own life.

Whether we are aware of this or not, we use inspired intuition daily, from developing ideas, undertaking projects, to managing our lives. Inspiration is around us, shaping the way we think, how we behave and even what we say.

Inspired Speaking

How many times have you heard someone speak at an event holding onto pre-prepared notes. Eventually the notes are put down as the flow of information is freely expressed and we say, "They spoke from the heart." We say, they have undertaken inspired speaking.

Spiritualists practice inspired speaking to bring forth information that bypasses logic and consciously known facts. The speaker may feel impressed to discuss a certain topic that do not relate to them at all, however the audience is captivated as the words are relevant to them.

Dreams

Dreams have a fantastic way of imparting important information. We have already acknowledged the dream about electrocuting cows that led to the special theory of relativity. Notably, Einstein had more than one dream. Inspiration came in a dream about flying down a mountainside. As the speed increased he looked up at the stars and noticed how their appearance altered. He later relayed this as the possibility for time travel.

No one could argue with the fact that Einstein spent many waking hours slaving over books, discussing theories and trying to consciously problem solve. With so much information held within his mind he would drive himself mad trying to sort it all out. Best just to do nothing, let logic and rational thinking have a break, and that he did. Einstein's dreams allowed for all the information he had read and theorised over to be subconsciously constructed into absurdly creative images. From speeding down the mountain to cows being electrocuted. The dreams allowed the intuitive mind to give voice and imagery in ways that scientific books could not.

Einstein was not the only scientist to attribute his work to dreams. August Kekule von Stradonitz was the German chemist responsible for the discovery of the structural theory of organic chemistry, including benzene. A chemical found in fuel, rubber and cars, just to name a few. The discovery of benzene came to Kekule in a several dreams about snakes. In the dreams Kekule recounts snakes coming together, coiling around each other to form a hexagon; the shape of the benzene molecule.

Music

There are countless examples of how inspired intuition is used and received every day. One of our favourites is guidance received in the form of songs. They may be in our head when we wake up or just come to us unexpectedly during the day. Many years ago, I kept thinking of a line from a song "I fought the law, but the law won." It was in my head every day for no reason until one day I received a fine for parking in a permit zone. Deciding to appeal the fine because the sign was hidden behind a tree branch and out of my sight.

I wrote to the council to request a warning and advise that they cut back the tree branch. As I was writing the letter "I fought the law and the law won" kept playing in my mind. This may sound insignificant but at the time it was important. Feeling justified with my appeal I kept thinking of how that song had come out of nowhere. Going over the words made me realise that part of me was aware the fine would have to be paid.

What is the point in having such a song? Why couldn't there have been a song that said, don't park the car under a tree? Even though there probably isn't a song with such words, my intuition was finding ways to communicate and incorporate the logical mind. Remember, I was already alerted to the song itself mentally noting that it was part of a message or warning which all made sense in the end.

Dreams, spoken word and songs are great examples of how inspired intuition can alert us to possible challenges or help us find the answers to problems which may seemingly take forever or not be solved at all if left to the old logic and reason pathway. Is there a way to turn our inspired intuitive meter on?

Writing

Writing is a wonderful way to clear the head of thoughts. Psychologists encourage writing or journaling to help with self-expression and freeing the mind of trauma. It is also a tried and tested method for connecting with the intuitive voice.

Writing may take on the form of a song, poem, novel or statement. The importance is how the words and meaning connect with you. Letting the logical mind go to unleash the inner self can fine tune answers, clear emotional turmoil and create a plan for the day ahead.

Developing intuition will have a profound effect on the information that is written. Receiving direct answers to problems or even predicating future events can all be achieved through inspired writing.

Art

Art is visually stimulating. An excellent form of expression for anyone who may need a little pick me up or reconnection back to creativity. An artist's intent may be to pass on a message or tell a story that can be interpreted in many ways and not always from the artist perspective. This demonstrates how art may incite emotions and thoughts that may have not been previously considered. By letting the mind go, the artist is free to express themselves through colour and imagery.

Just as dreams hold answers for us, inspired artistry is a conscious connection to guidance and answers.

Synchronicity

Coincidence is the term often used to describe random events that happen simultaneously. The sentient intuitive refers to this as synchronicity because nothing is random, everything is connected.

Synchronicity occurs as a deep intuitive connection is brought into the conscious mind before being manifested into the physical world. Examples of this include;

- Telepathic connection with another person. Thinking of someone days, minutes before bumping into them in the street. It is even better when they say, "I was just thinking about you."

- Decisions that manifest through sudden opportunity such as, needing a job and someone randomly states they are looking to hire right now.

- Asking for a sign that you may be on the right path. A personal symbol appears to you such as, a white feather falling in front of you.

- Seeing a sequence of numbers each time self-doubt creeps in or there is a decision is to be made. The phenomena of 11.11, 444 and other patterns of numbers are very popular.

Enlightened Intuition – Heart
"The truth shall set you free"

- Receiving accurate knowledge without pre-known information

- Wisdom – Beyond the ego to a place of non-judgement or emotional connection

- Free flowing living – obstacles do not become limitations to life

- Self-heal the physical, mental/emotional body

Enlightenment is the only word that can describe the connection with a higher state of awareness beyond conscious effort. The ability to know the answers to our personal life path and the needs of the soul exist within each of us.

For thousands of years, history has documented cases of individuals who have lived in an enlightened state of being; Jesus, Buddha, Mohammad, Mother Theresa were living examples of people who had access to their own truth. For many of us who are aware of their life story we may wonder what the point of having this knowledge is if we are to be persecuted or live a life that ends in seeming torment.

When an individual has connected to their higher aspect termed enlightenment, they can understand the actions of others and their circumstance without absorbing the emotional pain. We call it the 'bird's eye view.' Like a bird hovering over the earth to see the full picture before making a choice on where to land, the sentient can receive the bigger picture of why and how before consciously deciding on the next step.

Enlightenment also comes with a personal responsibility to respect the self and honour the body. It with this that we begin changing our tastes, craving natural food and desiring to look after our physical health. The changes are not forced, it is not about thinking, "I need to lose weight and join a gym," only to give it up in a couple of weeks. These changes are aligned with the natural progression that comes with this state of awareness.

Once the intuitive can consciously connect with themselves in a higher state, stress drops away and the fears that once held the mind prisoner no longer exist. Confidence, self-empowerment, compassion and understanding of life flow from living in a state of grace – that connection to our soul which we term enlightenment.

The outcome of living an enlightened intuitive life may leave old friends no longer finding common ground with your new state of being. Alternatively, they may hold you in high regard because the ability to see from the 'bird's eye view' can assist with guidance for many. Knowing when to offer insight and when to be quiet takes personal responsibility to a new height. People will always look for ways to find answers and often it is by giving away their power and failing to listen to their intuition. Speak with caution and refer them back to their inner guidance, help them obtain what you now know.

Do not think that reaching a state of enlightened intuition is difficult. In fact, the very reason you have chosen to read this means that your intuition is stirring within enough to make the connection with the mind and inner being. Being able to grasp feeling, receive inspiration and then to release the restriction of mind is the pathway towards enlightenment.

Now that you have had the time to go through each aspect with its form of intuitive insight. Pay attention over the coming weeks for any experiences that may occur. It doesn't matter how small or big you perceive the insight. Intuition can be subtle like a quiet nudge or visual sign. The trick is to pay attention.

CHAPTER 4

Physical and Sensory Awareness

CHAPTER 4

Physical and Sensory Awareness

Written by Kim

All humans are sensitive by nature, but when the mind becomes dominant, controlled by thought alone, we lose the awareness and insights of our being. We either come to live in the past or yearn for the future, either believing that the present is a stepping stone for better things to come or a burden that is best dealt with rather than lived.

There comes a time when past or future concerns become a burden on our mind, body and overall wellbeing. Throwing ourselves into work, family commitments, daily chores and routines to overcome the sensory expression of emotion and feeling can work in the short term, but eventually, something changes. A personal need to go back who you are and what you enjoy, before the responsibilities overtook life.

This is when many individuals take an interest in various practices such as meditation, yoga, healing and spirituality. It may be the practice is for personal transformation or a desire to study and become a practitioner. Whatever the calling there is almost always a desire to transform as fast as possible.

We have coached many who want to develop intuition to a deep level and expect to receive immediate, profound results. There is a perception that this can be achieved through intense forms of meditation or by focusing on the human energy system (aura), in particular the third eye or psychic centre that relates to inner vision (clairvoyance).

Meditation and inner vision is part of intuition – however without proper guidance from a teacher or mentor the individual may find themselves struggling to maintain a stable connection or giving up because the outcome is taking too long. Trying to jump ahead can lead to overstimulating the sensory system which will result in receiving confused guidance, overwhelming experiences and even physical reactions that the student could not have anticipated.

Accelerating intuition should always begin with a firm grasp on the current state of awareness. We can achieve this by connecting to our body, physical senses and environment.

The Physical Connection

How many times have you been in a beautiful garden or walking by the sea on a sunny day. Physically, you may be present, but mentally somewhere else, either living in the past or thinking about the future. When the consciousness is not connected to current reality then we are not anchored to our present state of being. We begin to have lapses in concentration, lack of clarity and focus. Eventually fatigue takes hold because so much effort is being placed on the past or future.

There are many reasons as to why we remove ourselves from current life. It may be that life seems tedious or overwhelming, we would much rather be somewhere else. Sadly, life can pass by if our state of being is feeling stuck and the mind is overworked by heavy thoughts that lead to an outlook of limited potential.

Connecting with intuition will naturally open the body, mind and heart to releasing the inner struggle that creates limiting beliefs. As our intuition heightens so does our sensitivity. Opening ourselves up to receive information from our environment is interpreted by our body as a feeling. An example is when clairsentients take on the emotions of others or even pain, causing confusion for the intuitive who is trying to differentiate between their natural state and that of external interference.

Getting to know what is a natural physical, emotional and mental state for ourselves is the key to determining what is intuition or a general aspect of wellbeing. Now is the time to open the awareness, so let's begin with the power of physical observation.

Observation creates a mental and sensory link with the physical body. The result will be lead to a deeper communication with the body and mind which allows ourselves to be firmly grounded with the present moment.

Take several minutes to focus on these key exercises.

Physical Observation – Focus on the surrounding room.

- Without straining the neck, what do you see?

- What do you sense? Temperature, drafts, feeling?

- What do you smell?

- What taste is present?

- What can you hear?

Take a moment to note the observations.

Remain lying or sitting comfortably. Bring the awareness to the body.

- How does your body feel? E.g. Heavy, tired, numb, in pain, aching, active, light, calm

Note down the observations

Continue lying on the floor or sitting in a chair. Bring your awareness to the following parts of the body. Do not jump ahead, getting to know the body may seem pointless or boring but it is an integral part of developing intuition.

- Head – is your mind in thought? Is there a light or heavy sensation?
- Face – are the muscles relaxed?
- Neck – is it relaxed?
- Throat – tight or soft?
- Shoulders – tension, weight or at ease?
- Arms – heavy, limp or tense and controlled?
- Wrists – rigid or relaxed?
- Fingers – loose or strained?
- Mid-back – tight or relaxed?
- Chest – can the breath easily flow
- Stomach – does it feel bloated? Tight or relaxed?
- Lower back – Loose, tight, aching or locked?
- Pelvis/hips – balanced, free to move or in pain?
- Buttocks – tight or relaxed?

- Thighs – heavy or light?

- Knees – weak or strong?

- Lower legs – tense or relaxed

- Ankles – full range of movement or limited?

- Feet – Swollen, light or heavy and in pain?

- Toes – free to move or stuck?

Did you notice anything out of the ordinary? It is amazing how many people either feel nothing new or experience sensitivities that had not been noticed before. Even the feeling of the heart pumping more than normal is an out of ordinary observation. It does not mean that a physical illness is present however if there is any concern it is always best to visit the doctor for a check-up.

When we pay attention to our body we realise how important maintenance really is. Eating healthy, enjoying what goes into our body, assists with bringing the awareness to the present moment. Even exercise is enjoyable, a simple walk to take in the air and refresh the mind leads to positive wellbeing.

One of the excuses that we hear from students is "I don't have time to exercise or make good food." In today's world, we have so much expectation that leaving ourselves until last is what causes the disconnection and lack of joy. Begin to change by giving your body a holiday. Make it a point to go for a walk around the garden or the block, look at what food is about to be eaten instead of just grabbing something on the run. Taking a few moments to look at what is happening is all it takes for implementing long term change.

Being intuitive does not mean you must be perfect but the sensitivity that surfaces will result in paying more attention to what you consume. Food and drink that were once craved may no longer seem satisfying, cravings for fresh food and water begin to seem very appealing. A desire to be in fresh air and surrounded by nature is very common for students of developing sensitivity. Pay attention to what you eat and crave now and take note if this changes during development.

If the excuses remain, such as I don't have time, take a moment to anchor yourself back to the present moment. This will bring clarity to life and assist with functioning on a physical and mental level.

Anchoring the Body – bringing back focus

This is a great technique for anchoring the mind, body and heart with the present moment. It can be practiced anywhere without anyone noticing that you are doing it.

- Stand still
- Take deep breaths in through the nose and exhale from the mouth
- Bring the awareness to the feet
- Feel the feet connecting to the floor (a slight feeling of weight may be noticed)
- Bring the awareness to the legs, hips and upper body
- Feel the weight pulling downwards to the floor
- Breathe deeply while paying attention to the surrounding area
- Take notice of what you hear, smell, see and feel

Practice this technique daily and before long you will be doing this at will without too much thought or conscious effort.

Exploring Physical Senses

We are part of an intricate body that is constantly connected to our physical and sensory system. The two work in unison by communicating or alerting us to all manner of situations. Unfortunately, much of the information conveyed is 'lost' because we are not sure how to process the type of communication.

Human beings have a developed intellect which is reflected by the vast and varied advances made in this world. Such important changes could not have been made possible without the dual sense of intuition.

Previously we have outlined the inner senses of clear; seeing, hearing, tasting, smelling and sensing. Now it is time to bridge the connection between the physical and inner senses into conscious realisation. To achieve this, go back to the physical connection of the body and realign with the present moment.

Stay mindful of the observations while we proceed to communicate with the inner senses.

- Close the eyes

- Bring the awareness to the breath. Are you breathing from the chest or diaphragm? If uncertain, place a hand on both areas to feel the where the breath sits

- Take in three deep breaths through the nose and exhale them through the mouth

- Focus on the rhythm of the breath, allowing it to take you deeper into the body

- Keep the focus on the breathing cycle. Deep inward breathing through the nose and exhaling through the mouth

After a few minutes, you may experience stillness. Sit with this for a minute. If the mind begins to interfere, go back to focusing on the breath.

- When ready and with eyes closed, imagine holding a plate of your favourite food

- What does it look like? How does it sit on the plate?

- Place the plate on your knees

- If you can, pick up the food with your hands

- What does it smell like?

- What texture does it have?

- Take a mouthful, biting slowly

- What does it taste like?

- Can you hear yourself tasting the food? Note the sound of your mouth or the way the body reacts to the taste

Take time to complete the exercise by allowing the mind, body and heart go to place of sensory delight.

Note: It is normal to forget what happened during an exercise. Tell yourself to hold the memory in the conscious mind, noting the sensory experiences.

CHAPTER 5

The Sense of It All

CHAPTER 5

The Sense of It All

Written by Kim

Instinct, inspiration, and heart-connected intuition could not be possible without the senses of touch, smell, taste, sight and hearing. These five senses filter information from the external environment enabling us to enjoy the sensations of the physical world.

With each physical sense, there exists a duality – an inner sense that is commonly referred to as the sixth sense. The purpose of the internal senses is to illuminate the inner self by activating the internal tuition that is inherently encoded within our being. You may have heard this encoding referred to as the higher self or soul. The higher self or soul hold the knowledge that we need for this lifetime, all the answers from birth to death and all that happens in between exists within. To access this information (with the right level of training it is possible), we develop our internal senses, intuition.

The information received through the internal senses is communicated through the body, mind and soul to bring guidance or direct answers. Intuition bypasses the intellect, because the ego is often strongly attached to facts and materialism. Individuals who lead strongly by ego are often 'in their head', forgetting the need to stop and pay attention to the creativity of life. Often the primal intuition, instinct may be the only experience of anything away from the head that is relatable. As for many others, intuition flows through to form instinct, inspiration and enlightenment.

For many of us, intuition flows through to form instinct, inspiration and enlightenment. Have you ever heard a song or smelt a scent in the air and suddenly stated, "That reminds of…" and a solution to a problem has been solved or great idea obtained? These are simple examples of how our internal senses work to stimulate the mind and heart into action.

Internal senses can assist with retrieving memories. If you have forgotten where you left the car keys, take your mind back to where they were last seen. See yourself in that space absorbing the scent, vision, sounds before watching yourself move away from the keys. The idea is to stimulate the internal self by leading you to the outcome of finding the keys. However, depending on your strongest sense, the result may lead you to feeling instead of seeing where the keys are located. If that is the case, a strong urge or pull may lead you to where the keys can be found.

Retrieving memories to assist with solutions is a fantastic use of the inner sensing. If a deeper comprehension into life circumstances is needed, then it becomes necessary to understand the nature of the internal senses.

Sensory development begins in the womb. From 30 weeks gestation, a baby can differentiate between tones of speech from mother to father. Today, many parents use music and speech to stimulate the baby in the womb as a form of early development.

It is amazing to think that a baby spends nine months in utero absorbing nutrients, sensing the vibrations of sound and making a connection to mum. What this demonstrates is the formation of clear sensing that will remain active long after birth and the likely reason many people state this sense as their strongest primary intuitive ability.

Think about when you receive a hug from a friend or loved one. The hug can invoke different internal sensations, from feeling love to completely uncomfortable. Imagine a baby that has not developed the ego to analyse and react rationally. A baby is open to pure empathic sensing. Picking up a baby when you feel frustrated or sad will have a profound effect.

Think back to childhood, did you know when your mother or primary caregiver was upset without them saying anything? Maybe you just felt their unconditional love every time you received a hug? Feelings can speak louder than words or body language.

Not everyone will agree that receiving feelings is their strongest intuitive sense. It may be hearing, sight, smell or even taste or a combination of all five. Most importantly, be aware of the experiences that are occurring within. To continually focus on the external world may mean missing the subtle signs of the inner senses.

Knowing Your Senses

It is safe to assume that there is an existing awareness of the senses, after all, they are used each day with little or no effort. Now it is time to develop the relationship and explore the duality of the external and internal world of sensory perception.

Individual traits are listed against the physical and dual sense. Which sense do you believe is your strongest?

Physical Sense – Touch

All of us enjoy the sense of touch but there are tactile individuals who use this sense to connect with the world. It may be that they always hug or hold someone when they meet or they feel so drawn to touching an object that they cannot resist the urge to reach out and touch.

Dual Sense – Clairsentient (clear sensing)

The sense of touch is known as clairsentients. Individuals receive feelings that become so strong they can interpret information just as well as visually seeing. The clairsentient will often be very open to their surroundings which can lead to a contraindication. When surrounded by people who may be draining, the clairsentient will feel fatigued and even take on board physical ailments that did not exist prior to the connection. The opposite effect occurs when in a positive situation.

Many of the people we work with initially believe their strongest sense is touch and feeling.

Physical Sense – Sight

Generally, we find that people who really look at their surroundings and see all that is within are more likely to be drawn to vision. Often, visual aids such as, colour and pictures are preferred over written text because the mind cannot grasp the information without the spark of colour or contrast. Visual people rely on sight to connect with the world.

Dual Sense – Clairvoyant (clear vision)

Clairvoyance is the ability to be impressed with visions of information. Many believe this ability is only used for predicating the future. While clairvoyance can offer predictions, it remains a wonderful tool for problem solving. Learning to clear the mind of endless thoughts, improve concentration and focus is the key to developing inner vision.

Physical Sense – Hearing

Sound is the last sense to leave us when we die and the first to be fully developed from birth.

People who have an acute sense of hearing can be overwhelmed with the various frequencies of sound. Even a dull hum can seem irritating to someone with sensitive hearing.

Dual Sense – Clairaudient (clear auditory)

A clairaudient may hear sounds that appear to be derived from the external world, as if a voice or music was playing. The difference is that there is no physical music or voice to create the sound. The clairaudient has heard this through the inner sense that is able to receive finer frequencies than what is heard in the physical world.

Physical Sense – Taste and Smell

People with discerning palates may find taste and smell to be a sense that becomes stronger when developing intuition.

Taste and smell are linked with stimulating memories and promoting wellbeing. From aromatherapy to tasting delicacies like chocolate, we value these senses.

Dual Sense – Clairgustus (clear tasting and smell)

The ability to taste or smell without physically eating or being surrounded by the scent.

Establishing a Clair Connection

Developing skills is like a child learning to walk and talk, everything is exciting. One day there is a discovery, an extraordinary ability that lets you hear, see, feel, smell and taste things that other people cannot. Are you going crazy (usual first thought) or is there an extra sense being perceived?

Extra sensory perception or ESP is what science describes as the ability to tune into unexplainable phenomena. What may appear strange or inexplicable now will in time become second nature to the developed intuitive.

Learning to attune with the inner senses requires daily practice. Letting the ego take a back seat while deep exploration is undertaken, let yourself go and enjoy.

Exercises to stimulate the inner senses

The mind loves to play tricks especially during intuitive development. Self-talk that leads to questioning the experience can result in loss of information. Before each sense exercise, prepare yourself by 'going within'.

Make sure there are no distractions from other people, phones, pets, or anything in the oven. After completing the exercise allow the flow to move into developing the clair senses.

- Sit in a stable, comfortable chair
- Relax the physical body making sure there is no tension in the back, legs, shoulders or face
- Place the left hand on the lower abdomen, just under the belly button
- Place the right hand over the forehead
- With eyes closed, take three deep breaths in through the nose and exhaling through the mouth

Clairsentience – Clear Sensing

A good technique to practice alone or with a partner. Pay attention to the change in sensations such as, temperature, tingling, pressure, discomfort. Do not read too much into the sensing, let the mind go and just feel.

- Place the palms together
- The fingers are relaxed and slightly apart

- The wrist and hand is not rigid but relaxed
- Bring the awareness of breath through the body and down the arms straight through the palms
- Repeat three times while keeping the arms and hands relaxed
- Slowly pull the hands apart until there are a few inches between them
- Turn the palms to face your chest, bringing them towards you but not touching
- Keeping the palms towards the body, begin to scan from the chest outward toward the shoulders
- Continue scanning the entire body

Clairvoyance – Clear Vision

Inner vision can be stimulated through visualisation techniques and tactile sensation.

- Bring the awareness of breath to the inner eye area or forehead
- Place your finger on the forehead, applying gentle pressure
- Tell yourself out loud that the inner vision is activated
- Close the eyes
- You may see a colour or the normal darkness may be intensified and an inner pressure felt

If there is no colour or sensation do not worry, continue with the technique.

- Focus on the darkness by bringing the breath to this area of the head

- See the number 3

- Look at the colour, size and shape of the number 3

- Hold the image for six seconds

- Let the image go

- See the number 2

- Look at the colour, size and shape of the number 2

- Hold the image for six seconds

- Let the image go

- See the number 1

- Look at the colour, size and shape of the number 1

- Hold the image for six seconds

- Let the image go

You may have noticed the number 3 seemed broken or faded or maybe it was strong for you. As the technique continued the numbers may have appeared stronger, brighter and even closer towards you.

Clairaudient – Clear Hearing

Clear hearing can be experienced externally of the body, just like physical hearing. The difference is that there is no physical being or object creating the phenomena, that is what makes it extra sensory.

Technique 1 – Stimulating Clairaudience

- Close the eyes to focus inwardly
- Pay attention to the breath by breathing in through the nose and exhaling through the mouth
- Relax the body, shoulders, head/neck, back, legs and arms
- On each exhalation feel the weight of the body going down towards the floor
- The body is sinking into the chair
- See yourself in a garden full of birds
- Take notice of the sounds
- The birds are splashing around in a bath
- Can you hear the water?

Technique 2 – Stimulating Clairaudience

Inner hearing is not delivered through the physical ears. It is the heart which delivers the sound. We will explore the power of the heart in another chapter. For now, open the inner sense of sound.

Begin with placing the palm of the left hand on the chest. Leave the hand touching the chest for the duration of the technique.

- Close the eyes to focus inward
- Pay attention to the breath by breathing in the nose and exhaling through the mouth
- Relax the body, shoulders, head/neck, back, legs and arms

- On each exhalation feel the weight of the body going down towards the floor

- As the body relaxes bring the awareness of breath to the chest

- Flowing through the arm to the palm of the hand is the life force energy carried by the breath

- Feel this energy move through the palm and into the chest, stimulating activity

Tightness, tingling, warmth or even coolness may be experienced. Energy shifts and penetrates to remove or alter any blocks of resistance.

Clairgustus – Clear Taste and Smell

Not dissimilar to clear hearing, both taste and smell can be experienced externally or internally without the presence of a physical stimulant.

Technique for stimulating clairgustus:

- Close the eyes to focus inward

- Pay attention to the breath by breathing in through the nose and exhaling through the mouth

- Relax the body, shoulders, head/neck, back, legs and arms

- On each exhalation feel the weight of the body going down towards the floor

- The body is sinking into the chair

- Keep the eyes focused on the darkness

- Let the mind bring in the awareness of a fragrant fruit such as an orange

- Smell the citrus overwhelming the senses

- Feel the orange segment in the mouth

- Notice how the body reacts to this stimulation

Replace the orange with something that is personally appealing for you. This may be chocolate, berries or coffee.

Common clairgustus experiences: smelling smoke, cigarettes or cigars, flowers and even tasting a bitterness in the mouth.

CHAPTER 6

Mindset versus Heartset

CHAPTER 6

Mindset versus Heartset

Written by Ben

It's a cold, wet morning outside as the alarm clock rouses you from the peacefulness of your sleep. You realise that it must be about time to get up as you look for the clock, as much as you want to pull the covers back over your head and will the morning's arrival to be delayed for another couple of hours. The clock confirms that your time in bed has ended; you've overslept.

A whole host of thoughts and feelings begin to enter your mind as you now think about having to get out of bed; thoughts about what day it is, what will happen at work, what clothes you will need to choose to match the day's weather, the list goes on. Suddenly there is movement. You are vertical. Somehow you have managed to get out of bed and stand up.

Although the process of getting out of bed seems quite mundane, seemingly occurring independently of your thoughts, a conscious decision has been generated by you to take that brave step. In the very moment before you began to move your body, a thought was formed to initiate that process. Certain parts of your brain fired electrical signals throughout your body to initiate the process of movement. In fact, hormones were released from organs and glands hours before, to enable you to awaken from your sleep. Our conscious mind is a powerful thing. Simply by thinking about getting out of bed, followed by deciding to do so, it happened. Of course, this is a relatively simple example of how our mind creates our experiences. Scale this process up to a more meaningful situation in your life and you can imagine how important your mind process is in generating the results you want.

An example of the power of thought and intention is the Water Crystal Experiments, the work of Dr Masaru Emoto. He believed that our consciousness could affect the environment around us, and that water was a natural conductor of that consciousness. His research involved recording the effect that words, music, images and prayer had on water molecules. This was done by exposing a sample of water to the conscious intent of the word, music or prayer, freezing the water sample and observing the water crystals when frozen. The results were astounding. Words, music and prayer of positive intent seemed to create amazingly beautiful geometrical water crystals, whereas negative intent produced muddy, irregular and misshapen crystals that often barely resembled a crystal at all.

The research also included taking samples of water from locations such as river and lakes, finding that rivers and lakes in developed areas would not exhibit the beautiful crystals that bodies of water in pristine, untouched areas generally provided. Some of the songs that appeared to affect the water molecules in a positive way were John Lennon's 'Imagine', and 'Amazing Grace', somehow reflecting the positive intent of the song. His research tells us that our consciousness, our thoughts and intent have an effect upon us, as well as influencing the material world around us. What if everything that occurs in your life is really a result of your mindset?

What is mindset? The definition of mindset is 'a fixed mental attitude or disposition that predetermines a person's responses to and interpretation of situations'. I'm guessing you may already have had an inkling as to the meaning, as even the word makes sense; the set of the mind. In other words, imagine mixing up a bowl of jelly and strategically placing jellybeans in the jelly and allowing it to set, locking those jellybeans into fixed positions. Luckily for us, our mind and brain are a little different and much more complex than jellybeans in jelly. In fact, It Is well known that the brain exhibits a property of plasticity. This neural plasticity is where the brain rewires its neural connections as a result of adapting to new information and experiences, ultimately changing the way it operates.

Mindset can be explained as a form of programming of your consciousness. In our modern-day life, most of the electronic gadgets we own and use each day run on software, using programming code to operate. The programs or apps in your smartphone or mobile device are coded to give a certain outcome, depending on what input it is given. In much the same way as these devices, our mind is running a program of beliefs and ideals, giving us an outcome or conclusion that is a result of the program. In other words, what you experience as your reality is based on your programmed beliefs of how you should act and react in life.

Are you aware of your mindset, your programming? If you were to record your thoughts, along with your responses to events around you each day for a week, you would see a clear pattern of how you act and react to life. Are you already aware of how you routinely react to events in a predictable, reliable way? Have those reactions helped or hindered you? It's a great simple experiment to see aspects of your mindset that maybe you are not aware of. It will certainly open your eyes to see just where you might be limiting your potential by thoughts and beliefs that are no longer appropriate for you. These could be beliefs that stem from many years ago, back in your childhood for example. It is natural that now as an adult, you may need to change or remove those beliefs that were once appropriate as a child but are no longer so.

As an example of the staying power of belief, I will share one of my personal experiences with you. Like many other Australian families, I was brought up on a typical 'meat and three veg' diet. Almost every parent struggles to get their young children to eat their vegetables. I remember being told by my father when I was young that I needed to eat all the vegetables on the plate before I could eat the meat. This belief stayed with me for many years, almost to the age of 30, before I realised that I was eating my meals in a set way. I then realised that I could change this. What was once appropriate for me was no longer required. You'll be happy to read that I no longer eat the standard 'meat and three veg' meals, as well as not being bound by a belief of eating vegetables before meat. I reprogrammed my brain.

The Energy of Consciousness

Recent scientific experiments have shown that there is a field of energy around us. This research shows that our thoughts, along with our emotions, communicate to and affect this energy field around us, choosing a reality out of an infinite number of realities that are possible. So, when you hear the saying that anything is possible, the following scientific experiments and evidence are saying that this is true.

There have been amazing discoveries in quantum physics in recent times. These discoveries are now beginning to explain the mechanics behind what creates our reality. The exciting news is that we are no longer seen as passengers in this world but indeed are active participants that can create our reality. To explain further how this implicates your current knowledge of life as you know it, I will explain in more detail.

The Famous Double-slit Experiment

Back in 1909, a British Physicist, Geoffrey Ingram Taylor created the double-slit experiment. This involved projecting light particles through a barrier with two parallel slits. The particles were then observed as they passed through the two slits. Science as we knew it then would say that the particles would travel through the two slits and remain as particles, producing two slits of light on the detector board. What happened though, seemed quite impossible.

Similar experiments with only one slit will show predictable results. The electron will pass through the single opening and land on the detector board as a particle, as expected. When two slits were used, the same particles did something very different and unexpected. The electron would pass through both slits at the same time, only as a wave could do, leaving a wave pattern on the detector plate.

The most likely explanation is that the second slit has causes the electron to travel as if it were a wave, then somehow change back to a particle after it has passed through the two slits. How did this happen? How could a single particle pass through two slits at the same time, changing its properties from a particle to a wave and then back to a particle? To have navigated in this manner, the electron would need to have known that there were two slits. Does this imply a sense of consciousness or sentience?

As it stands today, we do not believe that electrons are sentient or have a consciousness that can change the way they behave, based on environmental factors around them. So, how do we explain this? The common theory with this experiment is that we as the observer are the only sentient being present in that moment that has an awareness of the two slits.

This is where our current understandings are questioned. What if the actions of the electron are due to the observer's knowledge that there are two slits? This means that the consciousness of the observer is influencing and determining how the electron behaves.

In a nutshell, electrons may act predictably, but also unpredictably such as when acting like waves. When this happens, quantum theories are the only way to explain what is happening. Now that things are getting interesting, let's look at a couple of popular theories to explain and interpret the double-slit experiment results.

A widely accepted explanation dating back to 1927 suggests that the universe exists as an infinite number of possibilities. Take a moment to think about this as it may take some time to fully absorb the principle. This theory states that in each moment, an endless amount of possibilities exists. These infinite universe possibilities are undefined and without form until one of those possibilities is selected.

A possibility is selected and defined, through the act of observation and awareness by a person. With this interpretation, simply by being an observer, we can turn one of infinite possibilities into a reality. In that moment, all the person would experience would be that reality, their reality. Does this mean that the universe we know exists only if there is someone to observe it? Imagine for a moment what you might want to choose as your reality.

Another similar theory, the many-worlds theory, agrees that there are an infinite number of possibilities existing simultaneously at any one time. Where the many-worlds interpretation differs, each possibility occurs in parallel dimensions, called alternate universes. If one could travel between these alternate realities, they would experience a slightly different version of reality to what they knew previously. Imagine shifting your mindset and suddenly experiencing a slightly different outcome in a new reality that is similar but different to what you previously knew? The many-worlds interpretation suggest that we exist in each of these alternate realities.

A third interpretation, the Penrose Interpretation, further theorises the infinite possibilities universe. The core belief with this interpretation is that all these possibilities are formed of matter, unlike the previous two interpretations. Since matter has mass and mass creates its own gravity, each universe would have a gravitational field. The energy to maintain these versions of the universe would be so great that they would eventually collapse into just one possibility, which would be the version we term as our reality.

To recap, the double-slit experiment has shown that we, as observers, can influence matter around us simply by being an observer. Interpretations of this experiment theorise that there are many or even an infinite amount of variations of the universe or our version of reality as we know it and by consciously focusing our attention on an event, we choose one those realities. Is it simply a matter of thinking about a different possibility and wishing that it comes true that will give the result we're looking for?

Thinking about your life for a moment, have you ever used an affirmation to bring you the success, joy, happiness or health that you desire? What was the result? Can we change what we experience, our reality, simply by saying and visualising something? There is another factor in the equation, and it has to do with the organ in the human body that has the largest electromagnetic field.

The Heart is More Than Just a Circulatory Pump

Which organ in the body do you think emits the largest electromagnetic field? Take a moment to think about it. The brain? No, it is the heart that produces the largest electromagnetic field out of all the organs in the human body. The HeartMath Institute has pioneered studies and experiments to explore the power of the heart and the effect of emotions on the physical body. Naturally, their research was focused in the one place that our emotions seem to be generated, the heart.

I want to share some of their research that I'm sure will change the way you think about the importance of your heart and emotions.

One of their research findings is particularly fascinating. They worked out a method to measure and record the electromagnetic field that the heart generates. Just how large would you think that this field is? Try the following multiple-choice question to see how much you know about the heart.

The size of the electromagnetic field that the heart generates is:

a)   10 cm

b)   50 cm

c)   80 cm

d)   200 cm

What did you choose? Did you guess blindly or did you make an intuitive guess? The HeartMath Institute research measured the field to be between 150–240 cm. The measuring equipment they used was not able to detect beyond this distance, suggesting that this field could reach out even further. This field is in the shape of what is called a torus, but essentially resembles a giant donut, with your heart in the very centre of that donut. Imagine as you walk down the street or in the supermarket, just how many heart fields of other people you pass through each day, as well as how many people pass through yours.

Many years ago, in my early thirties, I was visiting a friend and we had decided to go down to his local supermarket to get some ingredients for dinner that night. I had not been to that supermarket before and remember trying to find the delicatessen, which was at the back of the store. As I turned the corner of an aisle, I noticed a popup stall in the aisle, where a lady was giving away free samples of a freshly cooked sausage that they were promoting. As I walked within a couple of metres of the stall, I vividly recall feeling an overwhelming sense of love and compassion; something that was completely out of the ordinary. At that point I had not even engaged with the woman. I didn't feel like a sample, so I ignored her. I turned and looked into the woman's eyes as I said no thank you to a sample of the sausage. As I was walking away from the stall I noticed that this overwhelming feeling of love and compassion began to subside. By the time I had turned the corner of the next aisle the feeling had completely gone. What I didn't realise at the time was I had walked into her heart field and was picking up on her amazing state of compassion in her heart; something very different from what I was resonating to at the time.

What exactly is this heart field and what does it mean in our lives? This next experiment conducted by the HeartMath Institute focused on the effects of emotions on human DNA. This experiment consisted of isolating human DNA in a glass beaker and exposing it to a powerful emotion. The participants of this experiment who created the emotion used techniques to quieten the mind, shift their awareness to the heart area and focus on positive emotions such as unconditional love.

The experiment revealed an amazing result. Through chemical and visual detection, the researchers measured and observed that a range of emotional intentions created an effect on the DNA, causing it to wind or unwind, depending on the emotion. This suggests the amazing power of our emotions and life-changing effects it can have on us and those around us, even the world.

More scientific research has found that within the heart muscle, there are brain-like cells. These neurons are not just for operating and controlling the heart muscle operation, they are also capable of both receiving and sending impulses to the brain, as well as throughout the body. This suggests that the heart and brain are connected and can communicate to each other. What an amazing revelation; the brain is no longer known to be the sole organ that controls the body. Interestingly, research into the immune and gastric systems has also shown that there are also brain-like cells within those areas, changing the way we look at how our body operates and functions as a system.

We now know that the heart has the largest energy field of any organ in our body, can change and affect living DNA with emotions, and has its own intelligence in the form of brain neuron cells, enabling it to 'talk' to the brain. All this research into the heart and emotions suggest that the way we feel affects and interacts with not just our own physical body but also people around us. There is a field of energy, often referred to as subtle energy, that connects everything in the universe. We also have learned that our emotions are powerful and seems to be the key to interacting with this field of energy. What role does the heart play in understanding our intuitive sense?

A study was carried out by Rollin McCraty, Mike Atkinson and Raymond Trevor Bradley from the HeartMath Institute to develop scientific understanding of intuition. The idea was to carry out more advanced work on earlier experiments that suggested the body can respond to emotionally arousing stimuli seconds before it is experienced. Another aspect of the research was to develop a theory to explain how the body receives and processes intuitive information.

The study was conducted by showing emotionally arousing pictures to the participants under two experimental conditions: a baseline condition of normal psychophysiological function and a condition of physiological coherence or state of compassion. Electroencephalogram (EEG) and electrocardiogram (ECG) measurements were taken. These measures were used to investigate where and when in the brain and body intuitive information is processed.

The study's results were amazing, questioning the way we understand the heart's traditional role in our body. The heart appears to be involved in the processing and decoding of intuitive information; the brain does not work alone. The study presents compelling evidence that the body's perceptual apparatus is continuously scanning the future as it appears to process information about future events seconds before they occur. The study also presented evidence that females are somewhat more attuned to intuitive information from the heart than men, suggesting that feminine intuition is a real phenomenon.

All the preceding heart research shows that the heart plays a much more important role in our body than just a pump for our circulatory system. The heart can communicate our emotions and consciousness to the world around us. I think we have known this within our collective consciousness for a while but have not integrated this in our lives. There are many common phrases that we say on a regular basis such as "they didn't have their heart in it" or "the heart of the matter", implying the importance of our heart in our lives.

The heart processes every emotion we experience, not only expressing this in its electromagnetic aura, but also keeping a record of these emotions. Consider the following example. A couple have been living together for many years, even decades. They have shared the ups and downs of life together, seeing their children and grandchildren grow and mature, fashions come and go. One of the couple dies. The person left to survive their partner suffers the loss of their loved one of many years, leaving them on their own. It is not uncommon that the surviving person passes on within a few months of their partner, either suffering a heart attack or undisclosed medical cause of death. When our heart breaks with emotion, it can literally break under the strain of those emotions.

From Mindset to Heartset

The conscious mind holds thoughts and beliefs that can affect how we think and act. The heart centre holds our emotions, which can affect how we emotionally act and respond to life – the term used is heartset. The heart interacts with the energy field and forms the connection between human identity and the soul, and as has been proven, is the source of our intuition. Truth resides in the heart. If you want the truth as to what is ultimately in your best interest, for instance regarding your life purpose, the heart will give you the unbiased truth. It is the connection to your higher self that knows what is best for you. That is why focusing on the heart as a centre for intelligence, asking it important questions about your life is more relevant than asking the conscious mind. The emotions held within the heart, the heartset, are like held beliefs in the mind. Changing your heartset is to change the frequency of the emotions held in the heart, including the pre-set ways you respond emotionally in situations.

When the mind dominates over the heart, there is restlessness and indecision. A good example is procrastination. When someone is unable to make a decision, relying solely on the conscious mind without consulting the heart intelligence, there will always be a sense of uncertainty or not being completely satisfied with their decision. As we discussed earlier, there is a link between the brain cells in the heart and the brain itself, so it makes sense that if the conscious mind is not listening to the information the heart is trying to share with it, then there will be bound to be inner conflict in the decision-making process. Strengthening your connection to your heart intelligence will not only help you with the seemingly important decisions, it will also help you with intuitive insight in each moment of your life, insights that give you awareness of information that precede the conscious minds awareness and knowledge.

Exercise in Heart Centring

1. Find a time and place where you will not be disturbed

2. Sit somewhere comfortably

3. Take note of your state of mind and emotions. Let go of any thoughts or feelings that may be lingering from your day. Imagine those thoughts flowing along in front of you, like leaves on a breeze

4. Focus on your breath. Take a couple of deep breaths to move your awareness to your body and away from your mind

5. Begin to focus on your heart centre, in the middle of the chest. Feel your heart pumping life-sustaining oxygenated blood around your body

6. Slow your breath down as you visualise breathing through your heart centre. Imagine as you breathe, your breath is flowing in and out through your heart area, rather than through your mouth or nose

7. Once this becomes natural, recall a time when you felt compassion for someone or something in your life. Feel that compassion in your heart area now. Allow it to grow and increase in size until your whole being is sitting in this state of compassion

8. Sit in this state for a few minutes

9. Begin to become aware of where you are and focus your awareness on your body, moving your hands and feet. Take a couple of deep breaths as you prepare to bring your awareness into your waking consciousness

10. Open your eyes

By taking time to make the connection to your heart centre, you will begin to see and experience life in a very different way. When we look at people who are able to see life very differently and live in a permanently enlightened state, such as Buddhist monks, what is their secret to happiness and enlightenment? What do they do that allows them to transcend the mind and our worries and concerns? They live in a state of compassion. When asked how monks connect to something greater than themselves, how they attain enlightenment, they tell us that it is done through the technique of holding the feeling of compassion in their hearts. Not just thinking about compassion, but physically feeling compassion in their hearts. This is the key to clearing the heart centre of all earthly concerns which impede our access to enlightened knowledge, our intuition. Developing and clearing the heart centre is the key to living in the flow of intuition, constantly accessing guidance from your higher self that guides you in your daily life.

CHAPTER 7

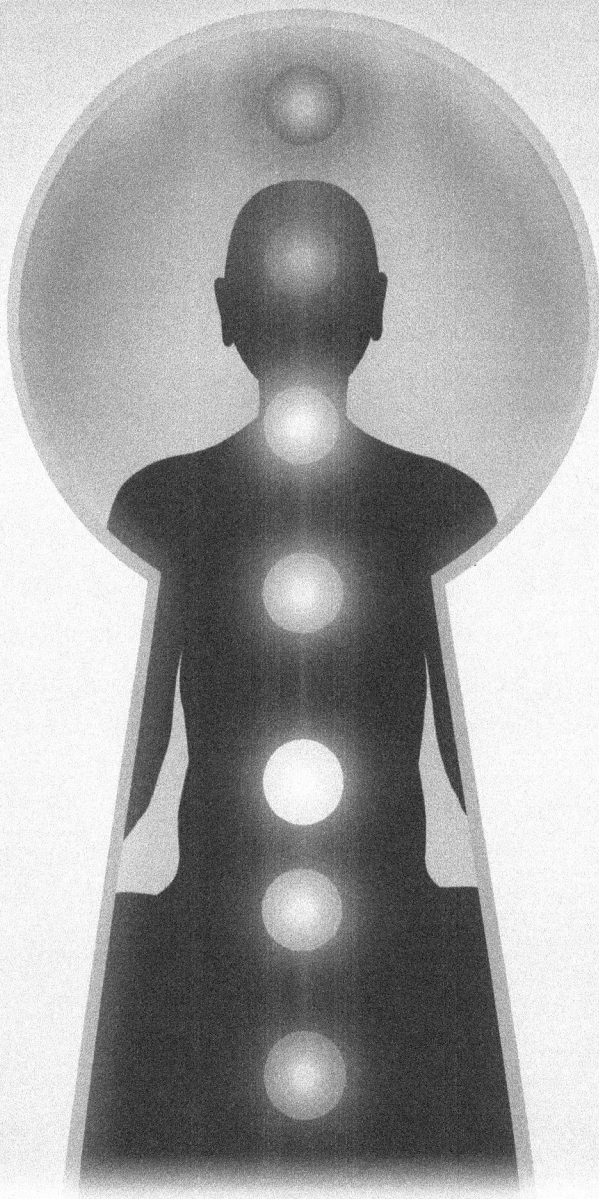

The Energetics of You

CHAPTER 7

The Energetics of You

Written by Kim

Before any builder begins construction, there is a need to study the architectural plan. The plans are drawn with certain goals in mind, such as, what is the function of the building? What is the desire of the occupants? How will the building adapt to the environment? The foundation of a human being is not that dissimilar to the concept of construction. Think of the physical body as the structure, and the desires of creation the motivator for how the building will function. The body and the desire would not exist without the intelligence of the architect formulating the plan. All life, but in this instance human beings, require the foundation to create the physical body and life path, however our basis is energy and the architect is us.

How does energy relate to us? It may surprise you to know that aside from having a physical anatomy we each consist of an energetic one. It is the energy anatomy that can hold an illness, days, weeks and even years before it manifests physically. We also have an energy field surrounding our physical body that holds thoughts, memories and experiences.

To fully understand how intuition works it is necessary to look at the energy anatomy and the field that connects us with all life forms. Grasping the basics of the energy system will provide key insights on areas such as self-healing, manifesting goals and understanding the why and how your intuition filters information. The last point is often the catalyst for individual undertaking intuitive development, because receiving inexplicable sensations or visions when walking into a room or meeting someone for the first time is very common. It can be overwhelming to receive such phenomena, especially if the conscious mind has its dial stuck on logic and reason. Why and how do we receive such experiences?

Much like the senses the body has a dual system which is an identical copy of the physical body. Known as energy anatomy this body is comprised from various energetic layers that go on to form individual maps. Like the architectural plan, each map has an imprint relating to the aspects that go on to form the physicality of life. For example, a map holds the imprint of all the physical organs, another holds an imprint of our mental thoughts, another displays emotion. All the maps come together, making energy anatomy the structural foundation for everything that happens in life.

In China, energy anatomy is widely accepted – one hospital, Huaxia Zhineng Qigong Clinic[1] is known for treating illness without medicine or surgery. From cancer to diabetes, trained medical doctors have been taught to work with energy, altering the pathway of illness and disease.

Unlike the East, the Western method of healing is to treat the physical body with medication or surgery. Alternative approaches are viewed as a secondary option and usually when the medical world is at a loss for a cure. Thankfully this too is beginning to change.

---

1   Huaxia Zhineng Qigong Clinic was closed in 1991.

Further research is being undertaken in health and wellness and the introduction of eastern practices such as meditation, yoga and reiki healing are making their way into schools, treatment programs and some hospitals. Hopefully, one day Western society will be open-minded enough to develop further energy hospitals like the Huaxia Zhineng Qigong Clinic in China.

Healing the body is an amazing use of energy technique and understanding – combine this with intuition and we have an amazing diagnostic tool that can heal. Medical intuition is the ability to look at the physical dysfunction or illness and relate this back to the energy anatomy. Everything begins with energy and the emotional, spiritual issues that have been held deeply are the catalyst for physical illness.

We were fortunate to be taught the art of medical intuition by Carmel Bell, highly regarded, and dedicated to the advancement of understanding the human energy system. One of the most valuable lessons that we were given; people will always go through the arduous task of trying to heal, believing that the mind is the answer, when it is only part of the solution. Years after finishing our training this lesson is always highlighted to me.

We meet many individuals who believe that they have worked hard to change mindset and overcome past hurdles, and they have. Many people come to us with a list of practices undertaken to better their outlook. We can truly see how hard they have worked and the benefits this has given but often there is something missing, the piece of the puzzle that prevents full happiness. In fact, one of the most common questions asked in an intuitive reading is, why? "Why does … keep happening to me?" or "I have worked hard on letting go, so why am I still …?" Again, the answer is that everything that happens in life is held within the energy system. From trauma to joy, the imprints are collated with each map of life. The physical and internal senses activate the imprints that become what are now referred to as patterns. Past experiences manifesting in various ways, affecting current reality.

The effort put into focusing on healing may have worked to some degree but if an intuitive can accurately sense the past as if it were a current event, then it is still actively affecting the present. The benefit is that an intuitive can link the past trauma/s to current events to show that the key issues have not been altered or eliminated from the energy body. Part of your being is still coexisting with past events. The patterns manifesting in life through, relationships, family, money, career, goals, or lacklustre attitude to life.

The energetic body not only holds onto the stored data it also creates pathways for releasing the turmoil into the physical body. Such pathways move towards the weaker areas of the body to create a lack of ease (dis ease), fear, or emotional instability. Using sound understanding of the energy anatomy along with the ability to alter the maps we can change all that is within our physical reality.

Claire is a great example of what happens when we alter the energy body to bring change to physical reality. Suffering for over a year from chronic throat and mouth ulcers, Claire called me out of desperation. The doctors had done all they could, aside from increasing medication or swapping it for another course there was nothing more to be done. Claire's business and social life was suffering. The pain becoming so intolerable that she would stay in bed and try to work from a laptop, keeping contact with the outside world by phone or email. Something had to be done, this lady's body was screaming to be heard. Someone needed to interpret the message.

When I met Claire, I instantly looked past her physical appearance and straight into the energy map. It was clear what was wrong and what needed to be done, but the hard work is demonstrating this to a client. Human beings still need proof that physical illness always begins with energy long before it hits the body. Without just coming out with this explanation, the process of bringing the findings to Claire had be done in a logical manner for her to acknowledge and understand.

We began by discussing how boredom with current life had stemmed from achieving her goal of financial freedom. Claire's business had reached its peak for her. Looking further, we discussed how Claire had always worked hard and just like a good girl had been happy and nice (outwardly) while harbouring her angst towards life. Claire had a failed marriage, her husband cheating more than once, but she put up with it and even tried to have both attend counselling. As we talked her energy would light up or sometimes shrink and even flash different colours. I watched the light show waiting for the discussion to highlight the reference points in her system that were causing the ulcers. When the colours in energy are displayed they can highlight key physical areas in the body that display weakness and disease. Energy never lies and what I was viewing demonstrated her need to please to obtain a 'good' life. The dance around the inner need had led to choices that were badly handled, resulting in heartbreak. Claire acknowledged her current boredom with life and that was enough to have a shift in the energy anatomy.

Prior to the session Claire was informed that the ulcers may be antagonised before the positive effect of healing to sooth and eliminate them would be reached. Claire phoned two days after the session to tell me when she went home that night she unpacked her wedding dress. (She had moved to a new house twice since the divorce and never thought of parting with the dress until that night.) Sobbing into the phone she had relayed the feelings of overwhelming anger that ended with a pair of scissors ripping the dress to strips before burning it in the bathtub. The purpose of the call was to book another session.

During the second session, her energy had indeed shifted but the underlying issue was still present. Claire's had a need to be loved and supported at whatever cost. Not limited to placing herself second in personal relationships, Claire would do the same in all aspects of life. In business, she placed her client's needs over hers to such a detriment that she physically could not see them anymore because of the ulcers.

We talked about relationships with people and once again Claire's energy exploded with colour and intensity. The controlled tone of her voice and body language had shifted from the previous session to being highly animated. It was clear that Claire was letting go of the self-control that had become debilitating.

Ten days after the session Claire phoned to say she was in bed suffering with intense pain. The ulcers were the worst they had ever been. We went through the techniques she had been given which calmed her and the pain. I connected with the energy layers, knowing that this was all part of her way of letting go.

Within days after that Claire phoned back explaining that a strange sensation went through her that night, believing that it was the pain leaving her body. She went on to say how in the early hours of the morning she lay in bed feeling as though she was part of something. This gave her comfort even though it didn't logically make sense. I smiled because I was aware that her held pattern in life was to please others at any cost in exchange for receiving love. However, Claire never received true love, unconditional love with no expectation or strings attached, and this made her feel lonely. Thinking that she was part of something was the inner sense surfacing when all conscious control had given way. Of course, she was part of something, connected to something, but I let her speak. Claire went on to say that she was going to listen to herself from now on.

Six months later, we received a wonderful thank you email from Claire. After the last call, the mouth and throat ulcers had not returned. Her health had improved so much that Claire had made the decision to move interstate. The need for the current business waned, but she decided to keep a small select group of clients while achieving her new goal, to open a café. Completely different to the work previously undertaken but it made sense. Claire had a desire to be creative, she loved people. The café would be a release for her creativity while allowing her to nurture herself and others. The move interstate was to a country area with a focus on community, that was what Claire craved, a solid heartfelt foundation and connection to people.

Claire's desperation for help led to bypassing the intellect. Finding us on the internet she went with her initial feelings and made the call for help. Claire needed little or no understanding of energy anatomy or maps, all she needed to do was allow herself to truly heal.

The power of energy exists alongside our inner truth. When we push aside personal needs, bury grief or resentment we are lying to ourselves. Creating a belief; if it's too painful don't think about it or just keep going and everything will be okay. Having the strength to be true to heart means that our body, both energetic and physical will benefit in so many ways. Little did Claire know that healing her body would result in overhauling her entire life.

We don't have to wait until our body is in such pain that desperation is the only drive for seeking help. We can alter our energy body whenever we want and benefit from improved health, vitality and openness to opportunities. We just need to grasp the basics.

Introducing the Aura, Chakra System

Each one of us has an aura, emitting a magnificent array of pulsating light that encompasses the physical body. Consisting of varied colour frequencies, this light forms a field of continuous flowing energy that acts as a filter between the external environment and our being.

The aura interweaves with the physical body to activate, transfer, or eliminate pathways that form all manner of physical, emotional and mental expressions. Each cell of our body is surrounded with energy that responds to the data collected from our external environment. Interactions with others, responses to daily events, EVERYTHING that we experience is processed through a system of storage units known as chakras.

Human beings have seven major chakras, aligning from the top of the head straight down through the torso before completing at the base of the body (between the legs). The chakras and aura share the important task of linking each of us to our human identity, name and personality and spiritual self, the part of us that remains connected to the source of creation.

Based on how we respond to life events, each chakra may alter in size, colour and intensity. With so much going through this system it is no wonder that chakras become overworked or underutilised.

We advise students of intuition to take it slowly when undertaking an advanced connection with the chakras. Unfortunately, there are many people who attempt training without any guidance from a teacher or real understanding of how powerful the aura and chakra system can be, unless someone has gone through an undertaking of energy awareness, i.e. demonstrated by Claire's case study.

The majority of people hold the belief that if it exists in an energetic form there is no need to worry. What they do not understand is that energy is the creation of the physical world that includes us. Focusing on one chakra by forcing it into overaction can lead to a decrease in results.

Anna, a sole practitioner of intuition is a great example of what can happen when an overzealous student tries to achieve immediate results. Desperate to develop inner vision, Anna decided to concentrate on opening the third eye chakra. Associated with clairvoyance and *inner vision*, this chakra is located on the forehead.

Although, very good at sensing energy, it was not enough for Anna, who became extremely focused on working this one chakra. Each day for long periods of time, Anna focused on various concentration techniques to 'open' the chakra. It wasn't long before she suffered from frontal headaches that became so bad she couldn't function with day to day activities. Even taking painkillers did not work. Eventually Anna backed off from focusing solely on this chakra and learned a good lesson from the experience.

In Anna's case, the third eye chakra had gone from average activity to stressed and overworked. You do not need to undertake concentration techniques to achieve an out of balanced chakra. Many people have over worked chakras. Sensitive people who are generally empathic can suddenly absorb too much energy from other people that manifests as unexplainable physical pain or discomfort. Get to know what is 'normal' for you physically and this will alert you to when outside influences may be penetrating. Get to know both bodies, the energetic and the physical.

Highlighting the Aura and Chakra System

- The auric field is a vibration of energy which resonates internal and external of the physical body

- The aura has infinite layers connecting with the source of all creation. The source known by many names, weaves a connection between all living organic matter and the spiritual realms

- The aura has seven main layers, together forming the map of the human body

- The aura is alive, constantly changing, colour, size and shape in response to the inner and outer environment

- The colours created by the aura vibrate at certain frequencies much like a rainbow

- The aura holds all our information from physical illness to spiritual purpose

- Chakra translates as – 'wheel of light'

- The seven main chakras correspond with the seven layers of the aura

- The chakras act as gateways to the internal and external world of the human being

- Chakras are our storage units, holding data such as memories, health, life path

- Chakras can vary in size depending on physical and psychological aspects of the individual and therefore are not always circular

- Chakras work together not independently of each other

The aura, chakra system is a fascinating field of study. We highly recommend anyone who is wanting to work as an intuitive should learn a lot more about this system and how it functions.

Highlighting the energy system and intuition also assists the mind to open to life beyond the physical world. There are so many books to read and stimulate the intellect but until an experience is had much of the information stays as intellectual knowledge.

The beauty of the aura is that we can assist with seeing, feeling and experiencing its existence. I love to have people in class stand up and view the aura. It doesn't mean that you will initially see rainbows of light, in fact most people begin with viewing a whitish haze before relaxing the eyes enough to see colour. Everyone is different and viewing the aura varies depending on the subject and what is happening within and that includes you. Viewing the aura on the self is very easy so, let's give it a go.

The best way to observe the aura is with peripheral vision, rather than face on. The retina (central part of the eye) consists of photosensitive cells which become damaged over time due to exposure from TV, computers, artificial light, etc... The peripheral part of the eye is less damaged from exposure to these elements and therefore remains the best way to view the energy field.

You can practice on a partner or yourself, either way try to have a plain-coloured background of white or light colour. If the background has a hue to its colour, then take this into consideration.

Many books state that it is necessary to focus on the individual's head or third eye area for the best results. In our experience, we find that the shoulders are a good place to start because the view is not directly on the face of the individual, rather to the side.

Viewing the Aura

- Stay focused on the area of the body for at least ten seconds. At this point you will notice a line of white/light blue/grey tightly surrounding the physical body

- When the haze of light appears, move the eyes slowly out from the body until the light disappears or changes colour

- Relax the eyes, blinking if necessary

- Begin again, increasing the time

Viewing Your Own Energy Field

It is possible to see your own energy field. Just look in a mirror or sit on the floor with your legs stretched out in front of you, your back supported with a pillow or chair.

Again, find a point such as your feet, using the peripheral vision concentrate for ten seconds until you can see the haze of auric body.

Keep practicing and remember that energy follows thought and awareness therefore we focus on the upper body. Most people live in the upper half or, as I refer to it, living on the mental plane rather than feeling. It may be necessary to pull your energy down through the legs anchoring to the earth to obtain a clear view.

Athletes are fascinating because they are always (almost) anchored. Their energy goes right to the feet and that's because the focus on the body, pushing to its limit.

Note: It is a common occurrence when looking at the auric field for the eyes to become accustomed to the energy. Often when looking away from the physical body the imprint of the field will remain on the retina, therefore you may see the outline of the physical body against other backgrounds. The image may last up to 60 seconds, or with constant blinking may dissipate earlier. (Don't worry you are not seeing things.)

Do not worry if you cannot see the aura. Some people are more tactile than visual it does not matter, one is not better than the other, both achieve the same result. Sensing and feeling the energy is as important as seeing. First, sensitising the palms of the hands.

Sensitising the Palm Centres

Begin by sitting on a comfortable chair.

- Bring the hands together in a prayer position

- Focus on the breath making sure that it is coming from your diaphragm and not the chest

- Take three deep breaths, inhaling through the nose, exhaling through the mouth

- Set your focus on the palm of each hand

- Feel the breath move through the body and into the palms – repeat this a few times

- Mentally note how it feels such as the degree of heat or coolness

- Gently pull the hands apart. Keep a space of approximately 6 cm between them

- Slowly push them together again, taking note of any feeling between the hands such as resistance, tingling, numbness or temperature

Repeat this exercise four or five times, noting any changes.

Working the Energy Around the Physical Body

Your hands are now sensitised for energy work, making this the perfect time to begin working on the body.

- Leaving a space of 6 cm, begin by slowly running your hand up the arm

- Move to the front of your body, chest, throat, face, brow, top of head before working down the body to the abdomen, groin, legs and feet

Take note of any heat, cold, tingling, and numbness sensations.

Do not be concerned about the sensations. You are feeling and becoming aware of your energetic body.

Energy Transference

We live and breathe energy, so of course, it is going to intercept other beings, including ourselves. It is the frequency of the energy that becomes noticeable. Human consciousness is a developed form of energy, it may choose to continue advancing, or it may become stagnant. Either way, consciousness alters the frequency to suit its outcome.

We cannot forget that other life forms, such as sea life, coral and oysters rely on the moon's energy to spawn. Trees and plants depend on the sun to thrive, transferring food to energy.

Intuition is used by sentient beings as communication between the internal self and external environment, including the ability to reach other forms of existence. Those who are extra sensitive will be attuned to receiving the various energy transfers that stem from the material and non-physical worlds. Sensitives are like radios who require fine tuning, or else they pick up too many signals that cause confusion. Many sensitives are processing environmental information, stuff that is not theirs, taking on energetic debris that can lead to feeling weighted. In an unconscious attempt to clear themselves they will often go off alone, seeking solitude, away from too much interference. If sensitives learn to alter the frequency of energy, they can create a positive high-functioning system that will be receptive to life.

There are many people who do not see themselves as highly sensitive, but this does not mean that they are immune from intercepting energy. The impact may be expressed as out of character emotions, thought, or even dreams. Leaving the individual to question their mental state, stress levels or book a session with an intuitive.

Working as an intuitive and having clairvoyance as a key ability enables me to sense and see energy but this does not mean that I am immune to the effects. In the early days, long before I was aware that intuition existed, I knew nothing about energy or spirituality. I was just a child who seemed to get sick a lot or experience weird happenings wherever I went. As I grew I learned that there was a world beyond the physical that many people knew about but very few talked about. I began to research this elusive area and found the answer to why I sometimes felt odd or thought strange things and why I could see light around plants, objects and even people. The discovery led to creating techniques to help me harness the energies that were all around. When I began to practice collecting energy into myself I would feel better, stronger. Occasionally it didn't work and

I would feel far from good, so I learned to change that type of energy we feel as 'negative.' I also began to play with the energy by testing my intuition.

It didn't take long before I would be a few seconds ahead of what was going to happen in the physical world. Little things such as walking towards a telephone just before it rang or thinking of someone I hadn't seen for a while, only to bump into them at the most unlikely of places. Years later when I began working as a psychic I would meet so many people who had similar experiences but never told anyone.

Now, I see that my small happenings were part of something much bigger and very common. Energy transference happens every day. It is the reason you take an instant dislike or like to someone before they have even spoken. Who could forget the most common relationship quirk, saying something in unison with your partner?

We are often approached at seminars by health practitioners who openly discuss taking on the physical pain of their patients, only to have it disappear when they stop thinking of them or walk away. One massage practitioner used to say that if someone came in to relieve a headache then she would have their pain by the end of the session and the client left the session feeling great.

Energy transfer is so common that we included a demonstration of its effect with students of intuition. The group exercise involved the students seeing the effect that energy transference has on the physical and emotional body.

The exercise had one person leave the room while the remainder collectively agree to express an emotion. The emotion cannot be verbally communicated, the group must feel it, think it and be in the moment.

The group forms a circle around the unsuspecting individual who is blindfolded in case body language gives anything away. In the first attempt, the emotion was love. The group encouraged to think of unconditional love, maybe received from a parent, child, spouse, or pet. To enhance their involvement, we asked them to really feel the love as they view the associated memory. Individuals revealed varied sensations from warmth to emotional tears. They were then asked to think of the colour pink, allowing it to surround the body and move through the legs and into the chest before outward towards the person in the middle of the circle.

The result of love being the focus for group consciousness was wonderful. Even standing on the outside of the circle, not expecting to be part of the exercise we received warmth that encapsulated our body, like a blanket had been wrapped around us. When asked to visualise the colour pink and project this to the middle of the circle the warmth immediately intensified, penetrating the front of our bodies.

The individual in the middle noted how she received an intense heat and tingling to the front torso, and the sensation of hands pushing against her back (no one physically touched her during the exercise). Everyone agreed that they felt uplifted and energetic.

The second undertaking was a little different. We asked that the same volunteer to leave the room while the rest of the group focused on the emotion, worry. Everyone was asked to close their eyes and centre themselves before thinking of a situation that left them feeling worried. To assist with the process, we added the colour of pale blue.

The group were asked to visualise the colour moving up the legs and through the torso, out the heart and into the middle, surrounding the individual. Again, we stood on the outside of the circle aware that the lightness of love had suddenly been replaced with waves of depletion. The vibe of the room had shifted considerably.

The individual in the middle also felt a heavy pressure weighted around the head and shoulders. Physically, she wanted to hang her head and hunch forward while the rest of her body felt heavy. She relayed the experience as "the weight of the world on me." The group agreed that the room now felt very different with some individuals commenting that they felt a sense of pressure around the upper body. Another individual stated he began to feel sick with worry but stopped himself before it became too unbearable.

Many of the group members were surprised by how such a common emotion could have such an intense effect on the body. One participant stated, "I carry this emotion nearly all the time and have never been aware of how it feels physically when compared to the lightness of love."

All the participants were alarmed by the results, which demonstrated how stored memory can have an impact on thought, emotion and the physical body. What everyone was amazed with was just how easily energy can be transferred from person to person.

Unwanted Energy Transfer

Such is the power of energy that it affects the way we feel, emotions and behaviour. The previous exercise demonstrates what happens when each of us receives and projects various forms of energy. We used words, memory (for visual stimulus), psychology of colour and feeling as the basis for creating the intention to project on an individual who had no intellectual knowledge of what was going on. The individual received a telepathic link that imprinted the colour onto her consciousness. An instinctual empathy was received by her body that expressed feeling and emotions relating to the group intent.

Our energy body is the unseen force that creates the connection that we have with ourselves and the environment, including each other. We can strengthen this connection with positive thought and intent if we choose or we can hurt or destroy. Knowing how to manage ourselves, when outside influences may be disrupting choices, is important for living a healthy productive life.

Developing the intuitive link will automatically increase the awareness of how people and places effect the general state of being. In fact, it may be that unconsciously, you deflect energy by using simple body movement. Crossings the arms or placing the hands over the abdominal area create an instinctive barrier of protection, blocking the intensity when it comes to 'feeling' the impact from an external source.

The mind will take on the words or action from another person, perhaps triggering deep unresolved wounds that will weaken the energy field. There may be many reasons as to why this is occurring;

perhaps it is a trigger within your field that has set off the exchange, this doesn't mean that you have intentionally said or done anything. When Ben and myself were developing medical intuition, we would have strangers open up about their deep wounds. It didn't matter if they were people in the supermarket or at a social gathering. Literally, people would talk about how their experiences were affecting their life and health. We both knew that this was happening because we were constantly studying the energy causes of illness. Intensely, aligning to the patterns of cause, effect and healing the pathways to change.

The effects of the medical intuitive included energy healing, all of which was imprinted within the aura; thoughts, scenarios, reasons as to how health issues occur, sitting on the edge of our being. Individuals linked into this energy, almost forcing them to purge their pain and maybe they felt better once the exchange was over.

Health workers such as, counsellors or therapists often report similar experiences. Perhaps you are someone or have a friend that displays a certain 'aura' that makes others feel comfortable enough to share personal details that would otherwise remain unspoken.

All of us, at some point know one person that goes over and over their wound. They never seem to resolve the issue, or they attempt to move forward only to find they are in a different scenario, but the issue is still there. Again, it may be that you are tired around such a person, lending your ear to their woes can be depleting. Often, this is the reason the bond between people severs, because they are sick of hearing the same problems or tired from being in an oppressive energy. Sometimes people do not know how to really alter their behaviour unless they are shown.

Techniques to deflect energy, such as using body movement, visualisation and positive thoughts are all useful tools, but we also need to mindful of changing the way in which we view situations. Being in the heat of the moment can prevent the reach of a higher perspective.

Relationships are a great example. Those times when an argument stems from whose turn it was to do the dishes or cook dinner. Commonly, the small stuff causes the biggest upsets. Taking a moment to stop, breathe and look at the real issue, which is not the dishes, will allow for a higher perspective to be unveiled. Deflect the situation, connect to the fire of anger or frustration, be honest, that voice of intuition will tell you what the issue is and then find resolution. The same voice will guide the situation to a harmonious outcome. In doing this we are raising our vibration to go beyond the primitive instinct of fight or flight. (It can take practice, but it does work.)

'Raising the vibration' is a common term used by many in the intuitive field. What it really means is to go beyond the limitation of the conscious mind to alter the frequency of the body, both physical and energetic.

Teachers of self- defence classes teach students to raise their vibration, by focusing on the abdominal area for strength and power. Bringing the awareness to this area and learning to harness the energy just before the physical exercise. The fluidity of energy can be displayed by a petite female breaking through a stack of wood with her hand. Intentionally harnessing the power through the abdomen before having this transition to the physical act, the last step in the process. Keep this analogy in mind each time that you feel afraid or weakened by an experience. The power to raise the vibration above limitation exists within.

Notes for Negating Energy Attack

Unfortunately, we are taught to fear what is unfamiliar rather than understand its intent, leaving many open to the ill will of others or a seeming victim of energy attack. The simple fact is, there are people that will drain your being, cause ill harm through negative thought, intentionally create rituals or spells, or physically say and act in way that is pushing the deep wounds to the surface. If that is not enough, energy not of human will, such as residual emotions, traumas or happenings that have remained in certain place, may even cause an individual to feel attacked.

The best way to protect yourself:

1. **Be aware of** feelings, emotions, thought and behaviour that you are experiencing – if any of this is out of character, then it may be that an 'attack' is happening.

2. **Do not analyse.** Humans like to know why, however spending time trying to ascertain the cause and effect may delay the clearing of the energy or intensify the situation.

3. **Fight energy with energy.** Like the demonstration previously discussed, love energy is much more pleasant than worry. Consciously shift your thought, feeling and emotions to positive.

If this seems difficult, put your foot down and say aloud "I will not take on this heavy energy. I am love." It's amazing what happens when we yell out rather than think.

4. **Maintain your bodies.** It cannot be emphasised enough how much the environment affects our mental and physical health. Nature is the best energy purifier. Step outside, feel the sunshine or be cleansed by the rain. There is no excuse.

5. **Technical devices affect the energy field.** In today's world, we can't do without technology but increasingly we are relying gadgets to run our life. Computers and phones are constantly by our side, affecting our intuitive processes. It is healthy to switch them off, detox from their use. Start by turning all off before bed and don't have the phone next to you when waking, leave it for later.

Aura Maintenance

The aura is intricately connected with our physical body, filtering external stimuli that can have a profound effect on our being. Strengthening the aura will create a stronger shield of protection providing benefits such as a good nights' sleep, increased energy levels and clarity. When the debris is cleared from this field a clear line with our own intuitive voice can be heard.

Technique for Auric Protection

Before bed and leaving the home focus on the physical body and breath. Remember the breath carries the life force energy through the organs, cells, blood stream and physical system.

1. Breathe deeply, exhaling from the mouth. The body should feel calm and relaxed with only awareness of any aches or pain.

2. Visualise or feel the aura surrounding your entire body, moulding its shape with yours.

3. On each exhalation, this pulsating field expands until it is half a meter from the body.

Be aware of its presence, a shield of protection that is with you 24/7. Before long you will notice that the little things that used to be a problem no longer are.

Technique for Auric Cleansing

The aura is a shield that may require cleansing from any debris that is carried within the field. It could be the build-up of energy carried from a workplace or emotional energy that is received from others.

1. A hot salt bath adding at least half a kilo of salt and 250 g of bicarb soda. Soaking in the mix will draw out any unwanted energy.

2. Sage with eucalyptus or white sage. Have the intent of clearing the aura as you allow the smoke to waft through the field, clearing away any unwanted debris.

3. Scrape the aura with your hand. Approximately six inches from the body, scrape away from the body, from the head to the feet.

4. Go outside and bask in nature. Be conscious of the trees, plants and elements that are clearing away any unwanted dirt.

CHAPTER 8

Understanding the Pathway

CHAPTER 8

Understanding the Pathway

Written by Kim

> *Human beings regard energy as an external source,*
> *something to help them exist rather than existence itself.*

In the previous chapter, we demonstrated the results of group consciousness when focused on one person. Highlighting the effects of thought and emotions on the physical body. We discovered the energy anatomy and connected with the auric field. The strength and function of the energy system illustrated through Claire's journey of physical healing that resulted in a complete life overhaul. Concluding, each of us is a being of energy divinely connected to one another.

The physical body is the assumed validation of our independence. We see ourselves as individuals with our own thoughts, creation and experiences. The physical world allows our sensory pleasures to undertake experiences that we could not have if purely a being of energy. When we allow ourselves to be attuned to the two aspects of self; energy and physicality, the way in which we live is altered.

We accept energy as the force that can either heal, create or destroy our physical reality. Recognising how our inner energetic system determines our external physical experiences can help to alter what is no longer needed in life and pave the way for the direction of our heart's desire. In doing so a higher perception is formed, the mind is free to view issues in a different light. Personal patterns alter – for example, someone who continually attracts either unhealthy relationships, financial problems, health issues or arguments will be able to observe the pathway that has caused such patterns.

Observation and working with the abundant energy source will realign pathways to emit a new frequency of creation. For example, the person who continually attracts situations as the ones just mentioned can now see how each issue pushes their buttons, detaching from the outcome by observing the physical and emotional responses. The observations open the mind to change and this is where the 'healing' begins. The mind initiates the desire for change while the inner senses intuit a new path of action that is then manifested as physical reality.

The patterns of that are revealed as repeated issues that may not have been present for an entire lifetime. The inner pathing may have changed due to trauma or altered beliefs later in life.

I always remember when I met Mathew. From the very beginning he stated how he had never struggled to attract money or opportunities, life had been easy going. Even when we met I could see this man as very creative, this confirmed when he told me about his garden design business that had won awards. Attracting high-end clients that provided financial stability did not surprise me.

When viewing his energy field, a direct line went straight through his system, from the mid-torso, up through the top of the head. I refer to this as the divine hotline because whenever this is viewed the individual is openly intuitive. Mathew validated this to me by laughing and reinforcing he didn't share that with anyone in case they mocked him.

Mathew's life was about to change. A business opportunity had been presented and instead of going with his usual flowing intuitive nature he decided to listen to logic and reason. Deep down he remained unsettled with the offer, however listening to the advice of others and knowing the background of the individuals who presented the opportunity had all led to the logical conclusion that this was something he couldn't miss.

I opened our conversation with why was he struggling with listening to his instincts? For the first time Mathew had felt that maybe it was time to go with the intellect, after all this offer could not be refused, it was a sure winner backed by reputable investors.

I thought this was odd for a man who had found success by going with the flow of intuitive insight to suddenly listen to the intellect and push aside his true feelings. Mathew is a very open person and he had not hesitation in divulging that he felt it was time to 'grow up' and listen to sense.

As soon as he expressed his feelings his energy lit up to reveal the pathing of guilt. Mathew felt guilty about his easy life. He openly confirmed this by saying that he always gave himself to others that he believed to be struggling either financially or emotionally as a way of eliminating the guilt from attracting an easy life. That was the lightbulb moment. Mathew wanted to know what loss felt like. He didn't want this on a conscious level but there was an inner need to feel suffering so that he could relate by knowing what it felt like to struggle. His inner pathing was going to create a fantastic experience.

Mathew was going to take on a business venture with two other individuals that he only knew by reputation. Mathew's instinct was trying to warn him, even I made several attempts to explain that to proceed would not be a good outcome, he would lose everything. Mathew laughed at this, saying that he had never lost anything and rationally he couldn't see how this would fail. He had come for the session because his guidance had drawn him here, but the head was overruling his sense of intuition.

Months late, I received a call from Mathew telling me that he had lost his portfolio of real estate, his wife had walked out, and the business had gone under. The business partners were untouchable. He could not sue or claim damages and all that now remained was the family home. The bank was knocking on the door to recoup further losses and the threat taking away the family home seemed very real.

Mathew had never anticipated how many people would desert him over the loss. It made him think about relationships and how others really viewed him.

Not long after the phone call Mathew visited and this time I could see a difference. So much introspection had paved the way towards a more meaningful life. During the darkest days Mathew admitted to himself that his marriage had never been a deep soulful relationship, he fell in love with a beautiful woman who he thought would not have said hello if he hadn't been successful. Unleashing the emotional guilt, he began to take stock of the people he valued as friends that were no longer around. This has been very painful as he believed these people were friends but again, deep down he could see there was no deep connection. Despite all that had happened Mathew was relieved to have gone through the experience. He could now openly see what that what he wanted in life was the intimacy of others to form positive, fulfilling relationships.

Mathew was honest with himself, realigning to a new path that reciprocated his desire. It began with a surprise visit from his son. The two had not seen each other for years. His son had always viewed his father as giving to others but he himself had felt left out. His son left home as a teenager in favour of living a rebellious life. Mathew had attempted contact over the years however it always ended in misunderstanding. Now his son had heard what had happened and made the first move to contact his dad. The tears in Mathew's eyes conveyed how much this meant to him.

As Mathew spoke about the loss of his business, failed marriage, and recent reconnection with his son, I could see the difference from when we first met. This time he felt appeased about his life, the guilt had gone.

The business venture was never meant to work but what came out of it was the experience that altered Mathew's life. Thankfully he could see this and acknowledge the loss could be transformed back to abundance.

It didn't take long before I received a call to tell me that he was back on his feet. It was no surprise that Mathew had been working on new designs that his former high-end clientele loved. Once again, attracting financial abundance. The real step forward came from his son who recognised that both had matured from experience to re-establish a deeply connected relationship.

Looking at Mathew's life, we can see the pieces of the puzzle coming together. View his experiences from a purely human perspective and we fail to see the reasoning behind what eventuated. The human viewpoint could perceive Mathew as being a victim of bad luck or prey to cruel perpetrators taking advantage of his generous nature. From the human mind we do not recognise that we have co-created the event with the source of creation to seek a 'better' way of living. Could Mathew have chosen an alternate path? Yes, he could have obtained the desired results differently but he chose this path to realign his purpose.

Mathew is only one example of how circumstances can be created in the physical. All of us have beliefs that are strong enough to alter feelings, emotions and the frequencies that form the energetic pathing that manifests as our physical reality.

If we want change then we must allow ourselves to be honest enough to evaluate how we are travelling in life. The answer will reveal how much external influences have shaped our behaviour and beliefs to create the person we are. Going beyond this, we connect with our truth, the heart of who we are beyond the physical demands of the world. Here we will find the answer that will free the mind from limitation, open the heart to guidance and illuminate the path for balance between our inner source of creation and physical reality.

Breaking down the pathway to understanding our own life journey opens the mind, body and heart to self-realisation. When the mind is conscious of choice and the heart open to truth, physical reality will express the alignment of the two through daily living.

To gain understanding of your own unique pathway we have broken down the steps as:

- Sentient Observation

- Self-realisation

- Release and Let Go

- Healing Body, Mind and Heart

Sentient Observation

There are many ways in which each of us react and interact with life choices and circumstances. The pathway of intuitive development will bring awareness to the sensitivity of our nature and how much of this we keep hidden.

Given that we are sensory beings, it is only natural that energies are absorbed like a sponge causing compromising thoughts, feelings, emotional expression or physical ailments. Let's not forget the ego. The intellect judges the meaning behind what others say or how they say it. The interpretation of what we perceive as being the message can alter our state of being.

Even the most resilient of individuals are not immune from external influences. They may appear to have a better handle on things, however life circumstances will reflect their internal pathing and true handle on life.

If you are reading this book, then there is a high chance that you are one of the sentient beings who are aware of their sensitivity. Sensitives are people who rely on their instinctive nature to connect with others. Feelings and emotions matter most to the sentient, prompting the desire to please and often at the cost of their own wellbeing.

The devotion to nurturing the needs of others will alter the pathing of the energy system and the frequency that is transmitted by the aura, producing a signal that may as well read like a neon sign, "Help Here. Just Dump Your Problems Before Leaving."

Anyone 'weighed down' energetically by life issues, will instinctively be attracted to the sentient's nurturing frequency. Even strangers will approach without hesitation and openly discuss problems that would otherwise remain unspoken.

Without personal boundaries in place the sentient will oblige with the interaction, leaving themselves open to vulnerabilities such as energy depletion, confusion with the relationship, worry that they attract strangers, and all while continually living unaware that their pattern of self-sacrifice is inviting this often unwanted attention.

Being a sentient being who is sensitive to the needs of others is not a weakness. Understanding how to work with the nature of sensitivity clears the pathway for creating greater life opportunities, enhanced relationships, personal wellbeing. All of this comes down to looking at our human identity and the relationship we have with our energy system, higher self and personal identity.

Exercise in Observation

Relationships are extremely important in shaping our interaction with the world. Human beings learn how to interact by observing people and this is carried throughout life. Despite what may eventuate in relating, if we distance ourselves from family, friends, or lovers it has an impact on our being. Look at the key areas of life and note down the following observations:

Exercise – Write down the names of individuals, not their role. For instance, mum is her role, write down the name.

Sit with each name and be aware of what feelings, emotions or physical reactions are expressed. It helps to say the name aloud.

- Friends
- Family
- Spouse
- Lovers
- Colleagues
- Boss

Career/Job – All of us spend a considerable amount of time in jobs that we know are not right for us. There are also many people who find their dream job or career. Whether you enjoy or loathe the position our pursuits have a bearing on wellbeing.

Exercise – Visualise the working day by seeing yourself present in the environment. Step back and observe how you interact with others, the space and go about your daily requirements.

Note the feelings, emotions, thoughts and physical reactions that surface.

Wealth/Money – Finances are a necessity to provide a comfortable existence. Money is always being created and can be obtain in so many different ways but still, most of us have an issue with how we view and feel towards finances.

Are you someone who views money as 'the root of all evil'?

> ***Exercise*** – Take a moment to note how you really feel about money. Be honest, are there any emotions that surface? Do you believe it is hard to maintain or even receive money?

Hobbies – Personal pursuits can become an addiction that ends up becoming a necessity rather than a pleasure.

Take notice of what hobbies attract your interest. What attributes do they share: i.e. exercise is adrenalin pumping it makes the body and mind feel good, painting can lead you to being in the moment, sports can be about stress relief.

> ***Exercise*** – What is it that excites and attracts? How does it make you feel? Does this suppress emotions or enhance and nurture?

Personal Pursuits - The trinity of body, mind and heart requires that we need to slow down sometimes to contemplate where we are in life or have been and focus on personal wellbeing.

What do you do to self-nurture?

Where does the mind go?

Self-realisation

The benefit of observation opens the door of acknowledgment that leads to transformation. Openly accept the way you feel, think or respond to people or events without trying to suppress this by distracting the mind or body. Be mindful of what tools of distraction are being used; food, alcohol, exercise or overcommitting to work is commonly used to suppress the inner truth from rising to the surface. Suppression is fear of coming to terms with what is really bothering us. Usually we avoid the inner need because we don't want the past to resurface or it's become easier to deal with life when throwing ourselves into another activity.

All of us at some point have gone through a traumatic experience, maybe even repeatedly. Who is to decide what we perceive as traumatic? Only us. Looking back at the trauma and feeling something whether that is anger, rage, hurt, grief or love means that the effects from the event are still actively playing a part in current reality.

Acknowledge the emotions and the mindset, because it holds the key to freedom. It is a path of discovery opening the door to why fear is held. Fear that can be reflected through the inner self-beliefs that are comprised of:

- Self-esteem
- Self-love
- Personal honour
- Self-belief
- Self-control
- Faith
- Self-identity

Take time to process the fears that are held. What aspects of your observations relate or push the buttons of these fears? Are you ready to let go and allow the higher self to assist with healing and moving forward?

Sometimes we are not ready to let go of the pain or resentment. It is a human trait to want to hold on. The more open and honest we are with ourselves the easier the path of fulfilment will be. Wanting to let go of feeling bad and live a more fulfilling life sparks the process of letting go.

I once gave an intuitive reading to a lovely young woman who chose to have an impromptu session. As soon as she walked into the consulting room and sat down, my higher guidance went straight to her pain. For so long she had seen herself as a victim of abuse.

The pattern was established when she dated a man who had not disclosed he was married. The relationship ended abruptly when she found out. That was when he divulged that he had a venereal disease. The hope of having children was taken away when the results for contracting this disease came back positive. For two years this young woman (only in her late twenties) had kept the affair and infertility to herself, until now.

To have this surface for her in the session opened the path of healing. We discussed the fear and pain of the trauma. The ability to acknowledge the lack of self-worth that she had felt led her into this affair.

A while later she came back to say that being open about her secret had given her back her personal strength. Discussing fears around life had prompted her to realise that she had allowed someone to take away her empowerment and trust in others that was preventing a fruitful relationship. Now, it was time to be open once more and focus on the path of trusting herself to make the right decisions. It would take time and maybe some help but this lady was strong enough to see it through.

Release and Let Go

Releasing trauma doesn't mean accepting the situation or person who may have caused the pain. It is possible to release the past without accepting the ill intention of the event. For example, if a relationship ended because your partner found someone else, the feelings of hurt, anger and resentment may surface. The mind will go over the event, thinking about what happened. Asking yourself, did I miss something in my observations at the time?

Go back through your life. Are there any heightened emotions, thoughts or feeling that surface in relation to an event? Is this uncomfortable or happy? Are you still holding onto this experience?

Going through the observation exercise, note how the body physically reacts and what thoughts surface.

Healing the pain takes place in the heart. The heart is the centre for interconnecting physical identity with the higher self and the source of creation.

- Create the space for the transition by bringing the awareness of pain to the surface

- Acknowledge the pain will no longer have a bearing on the present

- Feel the heart open to your desire for transformation

- The breath carries the source energy through the body releasing the pain

- Use the breath and the inner senses of sight, sound, feeling, smell and taste to reignite your being with a heightened love vibration

Keep the exercise simple. The main interaction between your physical body and inner self is what counts. When we stop distracting ourselves from the need of the inner self and allow for the process of acknowledgment, healing can take place. The mind, heart and body adapt to a new sense of wellbeing that is carried through every aspect of life.

Healing Body, Mind and Heart

The beauty of being a sentient being is that each of us have a continual flow of energy to boost our reserves. We can never ask for too much, nor are we limited to receiving the healing that is crucial to our life path.

Accessing energy is as simple as opening the mind and heart to receive. Something that I practice to this day and has helped me overcome many situations including listening to negative self-beliefs, feeling anxious or physically unwell.

Many years ago, I used to work in a male-dominated industry. I was young and nervous being in the presence of capable individuals, each with years of industry knowledge. My self-esteem button was compromised each time someone asked me to undertake a task, resulting in indecision and nerves.

The working day was long, sometimes up to 14 or 16 hours, but I had to prove to myself and others that I could endure the day at the same pace and standard as they did. I found this difficult, my energy levels would fluctuate. Thankfully, I had my intuitive ability to draw on. This had already given me a lifetime of knowledge with phenomena such as energy.

Reminding myself that I had a constant connection to source energy, I used it to overcome my emotional and physical fatigue. Finding a quiet place, I took a deep breath and asked my higher self to energise me. Taking note of how I felt by focusing on the parts of my body that seemed weaker than other parts. I could see and feel the energy surge through me. In seconds, my mental and physical fatigue was topped up with the flow of energy. Anchoring myself to the earth I had a renewed clarity and conviction. I was ready to take on any job.

A few of my colleagues would make comments that insinuated I must have taken a pill because I was instantly full of beans. I tried to tell them that I asked for energy to provide me with a boost. Of course, they found this amusing and chose to think that I had taken some drug. Sadly, most people remain unaware of what they are capable of.

Now I open myself to the flow of energy whenever personal work is required. Taking time out to look at life, how am I travelling, what do I not want and what is not serving a purpose any longer. Even if this is painful to acknowledge. I talk to my body, mind and heart to see if I am ready for change or why I am remaining in a current position.

Self-realisation is the first step followed by letting go of inhibitions, negative self-talk and linking this to the resultant emotional or physical pain.

Opening ourselves to the truth instantly brings awareness to the co-creation with the abundant divine energy. Mindfully aware of the heart centre, ask for the energy to purge any stagnancy, blocks preventing desires and be open to the sensations surging through the body. Pressure may be felt in certain areas, take notice – this may be the resistance to change that requires acknowledgment.

All the knowledge and answers exist within. Use the energy to bring forth the guidance and remember this is more likely to be feeling opposed to direct voice. Take note of the thoughts, dreams and life events that manifest around you. Everything is connected.

CHAPTER 9

The Art of Manifesting

CHAPTER 9

The Art of Manifesting

Written by Kim

Manifesting is the ability to create from within. Each of us does this daily, as evidenced by the food we eat to the interactions with others, but little importance is placed on the intricate details of life. Instead the emphasis is placed on fulfilling desires with the hope of finding happiness. The search for the perfect relationship, a need for more money or just an object of want has created an industry of books, movies, seminars and teachings around the process of manifesting.

The emphasis is to program the mind by focusing on the object of desire. What follows is a series of activities, such as creating vision boards, reciting affirmations and becoming aware of the signs that will lead to the end goal. For example, if you want a Mercedes Benz then cut out a picture, say a daily affirmation and the brain will trigger a response that opens our awareness to seeing Mercedes Benzes all over the place. The process does work because part of the brain wakes up to trigger our consciousness into seeing the goal – in this scenario it is the Mercedes Benz. As if by magic we see Mercedes Benzes everywhere, driving right by, or in the car yard, ads come on TV, in magazines, we begin to believe that manifesting does work. When in fact the car has not suddenly appeared, it was always there, it is the brain that has altered to expand our awareness. It does this through the reticular activating system (RAS). A small part of the brain responsible for filtering information that will stimulate the consciousness. In our case the mind has focused on a car; this is now programmed into our waking mind. The RAS has activated the physical senses to alert us to the presence of a Mercedes Benz.

The RAS is an amazing gatekeeper of information but this is the first step in manifesting. The RAS alone will not get you into the car, no matter how many cut outs of Mercedes Benzes and recitations of affirmations. Why didn't it work?

I remember seeing firsthand the disappointment from people who believed they had failed because their wants and dreams had not been granted. At the time I was offering readings from a bookshop that sold all the latest titles on achieving results with little effort. The books practically flew of the shelves as excited customers thought the solution to their needs would be found. It didn't take long before the same customers would come back in the store confused because they had done everything the book said but nothing had happened.

I eavesdropped on many discussions mainly about why people had not obtained their new car, house or perfect relationship. "It's not the right time," "I have to clear my karma," "I can feel it will happen soon," "I need to focus more." Unfortunately, the book did not cover what happens if your wish doesn't come true.

Rarely did I contribute to the conversation, after all, people have choice and many chose to read that manifesting will get you objects. I can understand why people interpreted the message this way but overall the message of the book revealed that each of us can alter current circumstances.

Eventually the day came when circumstances (or perhaps manifesting) allowed for my thoughts to be shared with another.

I was alone in the shop, watching the world go by while waiting for the owner to return from lunch when a nervous looking lady hovered around the door. She didn't look in my direction at all, in fact her hesitation quickly changed to assertiveness as she headed towards the back of the shop where all the latest titles were displayed. I couldn't help but watch as she scanned the shelves turning her head to one side to read the spine.

I was lost deep in thought when a voice called out asking if we had any copies left of that book that everyone was talking about. I knew the book in question, she had walked passed it about three times. I pointed to and let her know it was right in front of her but still she couldn't see it until I picked it up and said, "This one." Both of us burst out laughing before I could say that perhaps this book was not meant for her. There was a look of shock that quickly changed to understanding as I explained my thoughts on manifesting.

We talked about the premise behind the book. Our conversation flowing comfortably enough to allow me to share my observations from when she initially walked into the shop. I had noticed before walking towards the back shelves a moment of hesitation. Her eyes seemed to wonder along a different genre of books that made me think that maybe the secret of what she was looking for sat in that bookcase. I didn't know what was contained on the shelves, it could have been any subject, from tarot, ghosts, yoga or chakras. I was surprised to find a shelf packed with books about health, death and dying. It wasn't the happiest of subjects. I asked if the books meant something for her. Yes, her father was terminal, and both found it difficult to accept.

I could see the emotion in her eyes as she told me that her instinct knew that this part of the shop was where she needed to find her answers but her eyes were drawn to the back section where it was obvious the new titles sat on display. It didn't surprise me; her inner guidance system was attempting to lead her to what was needed. I could see her fighting the emotions (that moment when you want to cry but it's never the right time or place), but the book titles had pushed open the acknowledgement of the inevitable. Subjects on death included spiritual interpretations of dying with several books by Elisabeth Kubler Ross, a psychiatrist who spent many years talking to palliative care patients about their own beliefs and experience of dying. I suggested she have some time alone to allow herself space to decide if any of the books could give some answers. Thanking me, she let me know that this was what she needed to find.

I can almost hear some of you saying, "That is a nice story but, don't we always get what we need?" What about what we want?' To know what you want is great but do you know why you want it?

Behind every desire is a passion, this is the 'why'. When we can feel the passion surge through our entire being then manifesting becomes a whole lot easier. Passion is an energy that has the capability of altering our inner program to create pathways of obtainment. Let me share a personal example.

I always wanted to live by the sea, ever since I was a little girl. My mother and I would take weekend trips to the beach where we would both enjoy watching the ever-changing colour of the water and laugh at seagulls trying to steal someone's hot chips. I loved the trips to the beach so much that I told my mother that one day I would live so close to the beach that I could watch the sea every day. My mother asked me, why? I told her because I loved the way the beach made me feel, excited by the waves, happy to watch the people. That was my 'why'. The passion behind the 'why' flowed through by entire being without sensing any blocks.

My mother agreed that I would one day live by the sea. I asked how she knew, and her answer was simple, "You have a love for the beach and where there is love there is purpose."

Knowing 'why', connects purpose that incites the body, mind and heart to align, creating the result that is presented in physical reality. My passion for the beach resonated through my entire being.

Within a couple of months of deciding I was ready to move out of home I met someone at college who dropped in the conversation that they needed a flatmate. The location was by the sea so of course I took it. What made this even more special was it happened to be in the same area that my mother and I used to visit on a Sunday.

Over the years I have moved seven times and I have always found places in my price range that were by the beach and never with any issue of obtaining them. Today I own a home that is a five-minute drive from a beautiful beach. My energy is and always has been aligned to the sea and beach environment. The joy that I feel when thinking of the beach surges through me attracting opportunity and clearing the pathway to manifest its presence easily and obstacle free.

That is what happens when you are aligned with the 'why' of any decision.

What is your why? Why did you choose your career, relationship, financial position, home, friends? All of it is choice and if the answer is, "I just fell into this", "It found me", or "I had no choice", then what part did you have in saying yes?

Often our passion becomes disillusioned by held beliefs. The voice of self-doubt can hinder any goal, not to mention align our inner pathing to create what we believe we deserve rather than what we want.

When we make decisions, there is a process that the body, mind and heart use to determine if the choice is supported by our energy framework. For example, we need a job because bills need paying. Suddenly our thoughts go through the process of working out how much money is left, what bills are coming in and how long can current finances be sustained. Our 'why' becomes the need of a job to pay the bills instead of obtaining employment that is suited to our personal goals.

Manifesting a job is not always easy especially if worry turns to fear. Fear can override the innate inner senses that intuition relies on for conscious awareness. Negative thoughts are formed that can literally make us feel weighted by worry. The signals that we send to ourselves trigger self-esteem and confidence issues that flow back to our beliefs. The mindset of familiarity gives way to accepting what is given to us instead of what we feel passion for. The signals emitted by our being shadows the physical senses, the eyes fail to see the advertisement for a great job and instead only see the jobs that reflect what we really don't want but end up with. The ones that may as well say, "Apply now, start tomorrow, hate it by next week".

If we are not careful the cycle of change remains out of reach and all because we are not aware of the power, we hold within. The transition point for change is the heart centre.

The heart receives the frequency of the body and attempts to transcend this to the higher self to allow the intuitive responses to flow. Our waking body and mind may be too overworked by fear to receive the response from our intuition, instead it attempts to make contact in sleep through dreams or by catching our attention another way. The reason so many people see the synchronicities of life in numbers, music or simple words that seem to resonate from others is because intuition is attempting contact, but the rational mind is overriding the message.

How can we work with the heart to consciously create the space for manifesting?

The heart centre transcends fear to illuminate the truth but if the mind and beliefs remain in a state of flux, the individual will not alter the inner pathing to create a new way of being. The old beliefs will surface in a desperate attempt to have the ego rule over the heart. The intellect will justify accepting the job but the inner self, always connected to the truth, will make a choice; remain as is or take a step into the unknown.

The choice to stay with what is known results in the pathing remaining the same. We can manifest a new job but the work environment may be like what was previously experienced. For example, if the previous role consisted of an over-dominating boss, too much pressure to achieve results or colleagues that are not in line with our own way of thinking then this may be carried over to the new job. Different environment, new people, but same situation. The same premise exists with relationships, finances and everything really. Eventually a 'what's the point?' attitude is adopted that will reinforce the inner belief that this is all there is in life or maybe I don't deserve any better.

How can we alter the path? As we discussed earlier in the book it is important to connect with feelings. The mind is in control of ego, intellect and reason but the body is subject to absorbing the environment and processing feelings that lead to emotions. Let's use this process when we want to manifest changes in life. For example, if we focus on our Mercedes Benz, what is the 'why' behind this? Is it a sleek car that goes fast, I will be seen and noticed, a status symbol of success? These reasons have emotional needs behind them, what are your needs?

Manifest Your Goal

Insert your own manifesting goal.

What do you want? _____

Take time to look behind what the goal represents.

What is the real need? _____

What does it represent? What inner 'why' is held here?

If the aim is for a wonderful relationship, feel the heart and emotions. Open to the love that can be felt from another. Is there apprehension or fear? It's okay, let it flow through and allow this to be showing you what is the obstacle that has prevented finding true love.

Program the Mind

- After the 'why' is the process of programming the mind. Use tools such as a vision boards, or affirmations by sticking post notes over the house of your goal.

- Creative visualisation is wonderful for opening the mind to possibility.

Connect with the Energy

Never forget, everything is energy. Use energy to alter the inner pathing and create new foundations.

Be active and go to a location that may house the goal, i.e. a Mercedes Benz car lot, networking groups for successful entrepreneurs, meet-up groups if looking for new friends.

If you goal is to be success in business, choose someone that you admire that has already found success. Close your eyes and see them, connect with their energy and take note of the feelings and sensations that move through your own body.

Create a Physical Plan

I often give myself a seven-day plan for change. Beginning with the goal, going through the mindset programming, connecting with the heart and finally writing down what I need to achieve the goal. It doesn't mean the goal will be obtained in seven days, but the inner pathing will alter to create change and set the motion for obtainment.

See the World as Your Vision Board

Nothing happens unless we are ready to physically create it. Get out of the house and begin to see the world with open awareness.

When the ego takes a back seat to be in line with the heart our intuition is heightened. Pay attention to the inner senses, they may guide you to join a group or meet an individual that can assist your goal.

When we allow the energy to flow between the mind, body and heart we can see and feel ourselves in the presence of gracious acceptance. The power of co-creating between ourselves and the source of creation resonates throughout our entire being, igniting passion and purpose. If this does not happen then go back to the 'why' and the beliefs held around this. It may be that what you thought you wanted you don't actually need.

If it is difficult for the energy to flow, then perhaps the physical environment is not conducive to the goal. Be conscious of how you interact with people or places that may not be aligned with what you wish to create. Successful entrepreneurs surround themselves with success.

Sentient beings are sensitive to others by readily absorbing the energy of the environment. If you are looking for a healthy relationship, then don't go to a bar full of drunks expecting to find someone who is self-aware.

I use my passion for the beach as an example because when I close my eyes the senses are ignited. I see, smell and hear the waves, my body can almost feel the breeze. Consciously I am there drawing in the energy that is aligned with my manifestation. It doesn't matter if it is the beach or money, work, love or something else, what matters is that you are creating the reality that is aligned with who you are and what you desire to achieve.

It may help to begin with the small steps such as focusing on daily life. Be conscious of the goal and take yourself through the art of manifesting what you want to be aligned with. It could be as simple as finding a new place for lunch or meeting up with someone you haven't seen in a while.

Finally, let yourself go with the flow of life. Feel the rhythm of the inner self and it will lead to many places and people that you had never dreamt of. When allowing life to flow the mind appears less active but what is happening is the breakdown of the ego allows the heart of the matter to take over and when it does there is a guarantee of living harmoniously with all that is.

Manifesting in Simple Steps

1. What is the 'why', the desire, the need behind the goal

2. Program the mind into seeing the goal

3. Clear the blocks, allow the physical and inner senses to guide the feelings, emotions and thoughts around any obstacles

4. Align the body, mind and heart to the energy of the goal

5. Create a physical plan to create the goal - Step outside the door with open awareness

6. Go with the flow

CHAPTER 10

The Higher Self

CHAPTER 10

The Higher Self

Written by Kim

The various maps of life that form our energy system would not exist without first accessing the purity of our being which is known as, the higher self (HS). The essence of ourselves that has remained free of fear and limitation, deeply seeded with the source of creation makes the HS a divine limitless core of intelligence from which all lives are derived.

The HS is at one with the source of creation, drawing down to our individual being the aspects that will be needed for this life. Intuition is the tool used by the HS to filter from the higher consciousness to the lower state of mental consciousness. The intuitive forms manifest through the body, soul and spirit of our being to be presented as instinct, inspiration and enlightenment. The three form a trinity, bypassing the intellect to provide the various forms of intuition that were discussed earlier in the book.

To understand the union of body, soul, spirit we need to start at the beginning. For a few people it may take a little while to digest the information while others may find they already know this. Either way, open the mind of possibility and see the answers of life take form in all that exists.

Before each of us was born into a physical body, we lived as a light form of energy known as the source of creation, a divine intelligence.

The source transformed itself by dividing into beings of light known as spirit. The spirit is the part of us that transitions from physical death back to the source and again into another life form. Many believe that spirit and soul are the same. I refer to the soul as the energetic incarnation of this life and spirit as the essence of our entire being, transcending many lives.

If you do not believe in reincarnation that is okay, instead, think of energy as a dividing, transforming expanse that can never die. The spirit transitions to a soul when uniting with the physical body. As spirit we are in pure truth and love, choosing the parents and area of birth that will fulfil our learning. Allowing for the soul to feel the sensuality of life as an independent being.

There remains those in spirit who remain with the source of creation. They are light beings that can transform as a mass or collective of energy or divide into 'independent' spirits. In the West we refer to them as guides and angels however they exist around the world and go by many names. Their role is to assist human beings along the journey of the physical while maintaining the celestial balance of divine order.

Some of the beings have chosen never to be born into the physical, remaining as pure energy of light intelligence, while others have been human. We may have even existed in other lives with such beings who have then chosen to guide us on our earthly path. The reason I speak of this is to bring the awareness of life that exists in many forms, dimensions and planes. The higher self has access to life beyond this reality and therefore time as we know it becomes irrelevant.

The world of spirit exists on many dimensions, levels if you would like, to refer to these that can create confusion for our human mind especially when asking questions that are time-based. Think about those days when driving a car from point a to b without really knowing how we arrived at the destination. It's as if we checked out somehow and came back when the car stopped. The reason is our consciousness does move from the physical to other planes in what appears to be seconds when in our world the seconds can be an hour.

Many psychics have difficulty when viewing events that are time-based. What has happened in the recent past may appear to a psychic as about to happen, this is especially difficulty when viewing someone with senility. It is not uncommon for a psychic to see such a person as already deceased. Even able to communicate with such accuracy however the individual is still alive. The physical body functioning, however the consciousness can let go for the soul to step away and communicate. I have seen this many, many times and it took a lot of me to learn how to discern when someone is alive or deceased. There is a difference with the vibration, the soul has not completely let go to be at union with the spirit and source of creation.

The most memorable example of the soul and spirit connection was during my early years of practice. Each week I sat in a small class of eight people, all developing our various intuitive abilities. At the time I had practiced the art of spirit connection known as mediumship. Being a medium I would be drawn to people who had a strong sense of spirit with them.

Debbie was a lady with whom I always felt strongly connected to, but not because of she had a deceased loved one, in fact the opposite.

Debbie's mother lived with Alzheimer's disease. This only allowed for minimal communication, and that lacked any sense. Debbie welcomed the insights that I could provide.

Debbie's mum relayed events from the past and present, communicating with me what was happening around her and even the nursing interaction that was consistent, as she resided in a home. Debbie asked how her mother could do this. Our teacher advising that the soul is not bound by the body and it is very common for people with advanced illness to travel between the physical plane and the spiritual, reconnecting with the higher self and those in spirit who are attending to their needs.

When I communicated with Debbie's mother I always had a sense of being weighted as confirmation that she was still in the physical. Since then this sense remains as my confirmation with anyone who may be in between worlds. Eventually the feeling changes to lightness.

Another evening in class and again I was drawn to Debbie, however this time the room appeared different. I put it down to the lightbulb being on its way out or our teacher having prepared the room differently.

It all made sense when I looked at Debbie. Standing behind her with her right hand held out was her mother. I acknowledged her presence. Her mother told me that she had left her body completely and wanted to be here to say hello to Debbie in person. I conveyed the communication to Debbie who burst into tears. Sobbing, she managed to say that her mum had died that morning. The only reason she attended class that evening was to receive confirmation that her mother was at peace. I confirmed that she was and had been all the time that she was able to communicate to me. Her mother had stepped away from the pain of the body and into the full embrace of the higher self.

Since that evening I have communicated with many people in various stages of mental senility and those who are terminal, remaining connected to the body with assistance of strong medication. Each time there is a varying level of insights that reaffirm that guides and loved ones in spirit are there for us, while the individual themselves continue to observe life through both identities, the spiritual and the human.

Debbie's mother demonstrated the power of time with relevance to being in two places simultaneously. The body in one but the consciousness in another. For me to communicate with her seemed effortless and when relaxing into the discussion the appearance of time seemed to be seconds when in fact the clock showed half an hour.

What happens to us when time flies? It is in this moment that we are actively re-emerging with the higher self to bring back information that will become relevant, with time.

When life appears to be at a standstill, the higher self is busy assisting intuition to impart insights, ideas or to guide the energy and physical body with change. The saying 'the calm before the storm' is applicable. When nothing appears to be happening there is a lot going on. The higher self is busily co-creating with the source, which will result in life changes. It may not be the change that is anticipated, perhaps a clearing of the way is needed for our own individual higher good such as the ending of relationships, jobs or even loss of money. See it as an awakening, the knock on the head that is forcing the eyes to see what is truly needed.

The higher self will always make contact, and this can happen on a global scale. In recent times the phenomenon of sequence numbers have incited many articles discussing the meaning behind why so many people appear to be noticing numeric sequences, the most common being 11:11.

The phenomenon demonstrated is an expression of the higher self and source of creation, generating a signal to the mass conscious collective who are wanting a deeper relationship with life. This gentle awakening is inspiring individuals to go back to the basics of human interaction by using intuition as their self-guidance system to develop a conscious relationship with source and fellow beings.

It may take further nudging for the whole world to awaken but those who are now ready, and you are one of them will also notice the changes to current life. Perhaps old ways of thought are evolving in to alternative ways of thinking and being. Meeting people who are likeminded – and this may be a smile and eye contact – all of this is an example of the group consciousness giving signs that you are not alone, there are many who share and want to establish a coming together of heart and mind. If this is something that seems attractive but has not yet happened, then programming the higher self directly may be of benefit.

There are various methods to establish direct communication with the higher self. Talking to yourself as if with an old friend. I recommend practicing this in private, but you will find that you may answer your own questions during the discussion.

The art of stepping back when an event is invoking physical, emotional reactions. It is not detachment because you will remain aware of the responses and how they feel. Do not walk away from the situation or transfer blame or fear towards another source, instead hold it as if suspended in a time lock. Allow yourself to discuss the matter with the higher self by asking to be shown the experience from the higher perspective. What will be given is a complete picture (or viewed as feeling) of the occurrence allowing for the mind to process the information.

The same process as above can be used when the need to establish a pathway for living in purpose is required. Everyone has a purpose and we live this every day – it doesn't need to be found, however it is often how we are living our purpose that causes the disharmony.

Human beings are always busy with life so find the techniques that will be conducive for your daily living. There is no excuse for not consciously communicating with the higher self, it can be done anywhere and anytime, proving that the higher self and the source of creation encompasses our entire being, flowing through all that is.

CHAPTER 11

Peace Be With You

CHAPTER 11

Peace Be With You

Written by Kim

The higher self is truth of being, held as a vibration of love and communicated via the heart centre. Many hear this as the voice of the divine creator while see it through internal senses as a flash of white light.

The full embrace of the HS can last seconds, hours, days or years depending on the choice we make to either remained blind and ignorant to such expressions or to let go of the human traits that weigh our heart and mind to form the self-loathing which is outwardly expressed through fear and judgement.

To receive higher awareness, we must be ready to receive the truth. It may sound like a self-punishment, but I am referring to viewing life through the eyes of your own higher consciousness. To feel the emotion before standing back, to view the circumstances from outside of the situation, to note the physicality of being before letting go the tension. Standing back to allow the divine source to flow through and bring peace.

The hardest part of stepping back is to let go of the excuses. Blaming others or looking outside of ourselves for answers, instead of within, is to release responsibility and personal power that is a deflection of truth that takes us back to the 'why' of life.

Looking outside of ourselves for purpose becomes a distraction and an excuse for the ego to dominate our path. Letting go of what is happening outside and refocusing on the inner is to sit within the temple of pure light and harmony that is our being.

Finding the doorway to the temple is easy, sitting within to observe all that is within is harder. The noise of the mind can distract the mood while the physicality of the body prevents comfort. That is why embarking on disciplines such as yoga, meditation, intuitive development and wellness can assist with the initial connection.

Be careful not to rely solely on the classroom environment for results. If your connection seems to operate only during class time, then it is not working for you. That is the reason many give up because the energy of the class is conducive to the practice, but when the individual fails to create the same experience at home they believe that they lack the ability.

Disconnecting from the class illuminates the truth. The energy sat with at home is solely their own, therefore if it is lacking focus, feeling heavy or full of the fear and worry of life then this is the energy of the individual. It may be that there is no energy, void, again it is the individual. Realise, this is not a negative experience but the opportunity to reveal what changes required to establish a fully integrated connection with the HS.

It may be surprising to know that sometimes in the apparent silence is where the greatest insights are learned. The silence is of the heart and body, but the mind is often dominated by thought. In the West we rely on the mind. Do not try to silence the mind. Trying causes obstacles, the more you attempt or try the further the delay. Instead, allow the mind to flow with thought by consciously stepping back to view the display. Focus on the breath to disperse the source of energy throughout your being.

Being aware of the mind, body and heart of emotion will lead to a flow of life that is not forced by trying, resulting in the conscious embrace of the HS that will no longer require a class or time made at home to establish the connection.

Inner peace is lived when we are at ease with all that has happened and is occurring in our world. We realise that nothing is happening to us that we are not influencing. Knowing, feeling and living as a peaceful warrior will alter the outward world and all who live, bearing influence on others that need assistance or are already in the process of ascending their awareness.

May Peace Be With You.

CHAPTER 12

Enlightenment

CHAPTER 12

Enlightenment

Written by Kim

The connection to the HS and inner peace is what is referred to as the awakening. The realisation that not all is as it seems, life beyond the physical interweaves through life as we know it to be. Through the awakening the body, mind and heart transcend the weight of fear, loathing and limited mindset to a state of lightness and that is what is referred to as enlightenment.

Do not think that enlightenment leads to a complete dissociation from human emotion or thought. Quite the opposite is happening. The senses are heightened to view all that is occurring including what, how, when and why of our personal world. We will feel more, hear more, see, taste and hear as if all is new to us. Like a baby that can freely explore its world, a sense of wonder can lead to many various adventures.

Before we were awake the body, mind and heart absorbed the effects of outside occurrences, holding on to create the doubts and lack of trust. The enlightened being will transcend the experiences, taking from it what it needs and releasing this back to the source of creation to be transformed to light. We will evolve to a state of balance that will lead to living harmoniously with all that is.

Your journey towards the enlightened state of being has already begun and did so from the first chapter which introduced choice. We choose our responses to life and to how interact and view others. The effects of our interactions on our body has been explained and the process of inner pathing on the energy anatomy. Be mindful and keep practicing responses, thoughts, clearing and the actions that are taken in daily life. It is the small daily actions that have the biggest impact on change and transformation.

Next focus on the heart centre, the pivotal point for hearing intelligent source of creation as directed from the higher self. Keep practicing the act of compassion, viewing others without judgment and when this fails don't punish yourself, just let it go and program the mind that the next interaction you will be mindful of why the judgement came in the first place.

Enlightenment is not about going on crazy diets or undertaking hours of meditation in a cave nor is it beneficial to ingest mind-altering drugs. Everything has cause and effect. The journey begins with the awakening and follows through with compassion and a profound awareness that you are never alone.

When the pathway of conscious awareness and compassion are truly practiced the ego is overseen by eyes that see all. This is literally the ability to see the pain of another, the meaning behind words or to feel the finely attuned frequencies that vibrate throughout the Earth.

The journey of shifting the beliefs, opening to the new frequencies of intelligence will influence the mind, body and heart. A profound healing is taking place that will detoxify the entire being, meaning that physical, mental and emotional ailments will be heightened.

It is not uncommon to feel aches, pains, pressure with the chest or head as the energy is attempting to circulate throughout our being. Take note of the effects because it can indicate an energy block, a weak point within the system. Focus on the energy and direct it through by viewing or feeling it move the area, dissolving what was causing the issue.

I used to experience this as dizziness and stomach nausea. I learned to look at these two areas from an energy perspective, using the psychology of the areas that relate back to the chakras (storage units for our belief and experiences). I then worked with the energy to feel it move through both areas until I no longer had the effect.

It may be that the mind is screaming negative beliefs and creating scenarios that will validate why you should not let go. It is the last effort from the ego to hold onto what you have learned from the human life, the identity your parents gave you.

Don't give in, be kind to yourself and allow it all to flow through. Focusing on the inner self activates dormant memories that may surface in dreams through sleep or visions by day. The body may experience heat with no apparent reason, dissipating as fast as it came.

The celestial communion between the upper self and lower self or HS and human identity is merging as one conscious being. Allow the flow to be of guidance in daily life that will lead to new places, opportunities and people.

BONUS CHAPTER

Voice of The Soul

BONUS CHAPTER

Voice of The Soul

Written by Ben

According to the Bible, at the beginning of time, God said "Let there be light" – and there was light. The pages that follow this statement in the Bible give further examples of how God's words manifested and created all aspects of the world. The ability to create using the voice is a belief that has carried through countless human civilisations since well before the bible was written. It is only in recent history that we seem to have lost knowledge of the power of our voice.

What if the Bible was not really referring to God manifesting through his voice, but rather it was a symbolism for our innate ability as sentient beings to manifest? After all, it is known that we are all one and the same with God.

It is no coincidence that the voice created by vocal chords in the throat, is connected to the throat chakra. This energy centre is commonly known as the energetic centre of our will, our ability to manifest and create. When we use the voice to express our thoughts and desires, we project our will both physically and energetically to the world. We have that same ability to manifest events in our lives through our voice as what is mentioned in the words of the Bible.

The Voice is Linked to the Sense of Hearing

Alfred Tomatis, an ear, nose and throat physician in the twentieth century discovered that the cause of vocal dysfunctions in many diagnosed cases often stemmed from a previously undiagnosed hearing problem that manifested as a vocal problem. He theorised that "The voice does not produce what the ear cannot not hear", which became the hallmark of his work. This led to a further theory that information from the foetal ear stimulates and guides brain development whilst in the womb. He believed that auditory communication problems began in pregnancy, with the foetus not properly responding to the voice of the mother.

He developed the Electronic Ear, a device that filters sound to enhance the uppermost missing frequencies of the patient's hearing to strengthen the middle ear, to sensitise the listener to the missing frequencies. The Tomatis Effect was used to treat reading problems, dyslexia, depression, schizophrenia and autism. He found evidence that many of these problems resulted from a failure of communication, stemming from the ear's inability to hear certain frequencies. The Mozart Effect is a similar technique that uses specific extracts of Wolfgang Amadeus Mozart's music to help boost neural connections in the brain and boost learning and memory retention.

The impact of sound in our lives appears well before birth. It is said that the first sense to fully develop in the womb is the sense of hearing, with the ear becoming fully developed by the fourth month of pregnancy. Through past-life regression and hypnotism, people have been able to recount their mother's voice, as well as sounds that they could hear outside of their mother's body. If you ever have the chance to speak to a baby in utero, you may notice that they often respond to voice, particularly their mother and father, as well as the voices that they have come to know during their time in the womb.

Our sense of hearing been verified by many as the last sense to leave our being at the point of death. Many reports exist from people who have had a near death experience (NDE), stating that they were able to hear what was happening in the room the whole time they were unconscious. Without sensing or seeing anything else they commonly report recalling words from doctors, nurses or loved ones that are physically present. This phenomenon includes patients in a comatose state who have verified hearing medical staff and relatives talking in the room.

It seems that our sense of hearing plays a large role in our experiences, emotions and memories. Try listening to a piece of music that you know well and take note as the memories of when you first heard that song come flooding back to you. Listening to that song will also likely remind you of a special moment in your life when that song just happened to be playing. It seems as if the music is embedded in the memory as a vibratory marker for the memory itself.

The Power of Sound Waves

The power of sound waves or vibrations is currently utilised in many devices in our modern-day, probably in ways that you may not recognise or have heard of. High frequency sound waves are used to clean objects such as jewellery. An ultrasound device that shows an image of an expectant mother's baby on a monitor uses ultra-high frequency sound waves to allow us to see inside the body. Ships use sonar (sound navigation and ranging), which also uses sound waves, to see through water, mapping the ocean floor, as well as scanning for enemy submarines that may be trying to attack under stealth. Some animals have evolved to hear and emit sound frequencies well beyond the human range of hearing, using sound frequencies to navigate the world around them, as well as communicating to their family. Whales to communicate across vast distances to each other in the ocean. Bats use sound waves to see their environment sonically, mapping a three-dimensional outline of their location without the use of their eyes. Even our trusty family pets like cats and dogs can hear well above our range of hearing. You may have noticed how they are able to tell when someone is arriving at the house well before we can hear them arrive.

Sound is a form of energy vibration and can be measured by its pressure. There are many other forms that energy can take in our world, mostly invisible to our naked eye. Energy can be measured within the electromagnetic spectrum, as a frequency of vibrational waves. Just as current quantum physics research is adding to early theories from scientists such as Einstein, future research may discover even more about the fabric of our universe, possibly being able to explain the matter of the universe in even greater detail. The visible light that we can see with our physical eyes is a very small portion of the overall spectrum of energy radiated in our universe. The very matter that our physical world consists of, electrons, all resonate to certain vibrational frequencies, depending on their state of being, or level of excitation. Some of this energy we can see as light. Some energy we hear as sounds. Some energy we sense psychically, such as other living beings around us. The sounds we hear with our ears are just a much lower frequency of vibration to the visible light we see. If you were to break to laws of physics and slow down the frequency of light many times over, you could technically be able to hear it as a sound. When you go beyond our five physical senses, you are then able to become aware of the finer, higher energetic vibrations that are around us. This higher energetic state is the bridge to a higher level of consciousness that allows us to connect to our higher self and divine knowledge. This is the connection to intuition.

Going beyond our planet Earth, there is even sound in space, just not quite sound as you know it. Many of NASA's space crafts and deep space probes have recorded waves of plasma (ionised gas), radio waves and magnetic fields as they travelled through space on their missions. Through their instruments, they could modulate these electromagnetic frequencies down to the range of frequencies of human hearing. What resulted was astounding; sounds of the very fabric of the universe beaming through speakers. On the internet, you can navigate to the NASA website and download their audio files of these sounds of space that were recorded as these space crafts travelled on their lonely journeys out past the planets in our solar system.

Our Voice

A popular theory about the voice is that it is the expression of the essence of the soul. Computer software has been created that analyses the frequencies of the human voice and highlights any missing frequencies within the voice. The principle of this theory is that any missing frequencies in the voice highlight a 'missing' aspect of the person's soul in their current life and by reproducing and playing those missing sound frequencies back to the person, they will re-program and integrate the missing part of their soul essence into their life. This technique may help to uncover hidden talents or abilities that were waiting to be accessed. It could also be that these missing frequencies have the power to ignite a new passion and drive into a more rewarding and purposeful direction in life. This theory certainly provokes thought about what frequency we vibrate to and how new frequencies can affect us.

Think about the way you use your voice every day. When you stub your toe on the coffee table or jam your finger in a cupboard door by accident, what is your first reaction? Apart from a possibility of cursing and an outburst of discontent, the most likely outcome is that you would have uttered an "argh" or "ouch". The sound is a verbalisation, a manifestation of your response to the pain and shock. What if that vocal sound helps to reduce the severity of the physical pain you experience? Studies into the effect of making a verbal noise and even cursing when we hurt ourselves show that it appears that the act of making a vocal sound does reduce the level of pain experienced. The next time you accidentally hurt yourself, try to not make a sound; it is near impossible. If you can manage to control yourself to the point that you can resist vocalising your pain, take note of whether the pain level is different when you abstain from making a noise versus what level it is when you verbalised your pain.

Sound for Healing and Shifting Consciousness

For millennia, a diverse range of cultures around the world have used the voice, along with other sonic instruments in rituals and ceremonies. From Australia to Zimbabwe, the indigenous people of many countries have recognised the importance of using the human voice as an instrument, along with other sonic tools for healing the body, mind and soul. The voice is also commonly used to raise the consciousness, connecting to a greater awareness of the self and the spiritual dimensions.

Certain members of the tribes would use the beat of a drum with vocal chanting to fall into a deep trance state, whereby their consciousness would go beyond the physical world, connecting to the higher vibrational world of spirit. It was only in this heightened state of awareness that they would no longer be bound by their waking mind, allowing them to become a channel, a conduit for information, knowledge and healing energy from the divine realm. There are a small number of modern day sound healing pioneers that are researching the benefits and healing properties of sound, using science to verify and measure the effect of sound on the body and consciousness. Overall though as a society, we seem to have lost much of the knowledge of using sound and the human voice to heal the body and connect to our higher consciousness.

Sound healing is defined as the organic creation and application of sound frequencies, or waves of energy programmed by our consciousness to manipulate and change the vibrational frequencies of the matter that make up our energetic and physical bodies. This consists of our chakras and all layers of our energy body as well as the physical body. Sound frequencies can also change our brain wave state, raising our consciousness to a level above and beyond our regular waking consciousness, allowing us to sense and understand information that is beyond the comprehension of our logical mind. The power of sound healing gives us the ability to access and communicate with the higher frequency vibration of the higher self, our enlightened intuition, as well as to connect with energetic beings that are not of our physical world. Meditation or relaxation music recordings that contain focused organic vocal toning are much more effective at shifting the consciousness state than recordings that use computer-generated frequencies. A recording created with the correct intent will reduce the length of meditation time required to get to a certain state of consciousness.

As human beings, we naturally vibrate to a specific range of frequencies, in a physical world where all communication is made through energetic vibrations. Our journey as a spiritual being on this planet is to live in a physical body and experience the world through our senses; senses that receive, interpret or project energetic vibrations. On the path to developing intuition, your connection to your higher self, you will be working on a vibratory level that goes above and beyond the physical senses. You will become aware of limitations in mind, heart and body that will inhibit your ability to access your intuitive guidance, or even be aware that it is there in some cases. Sound healing is a process that we can use to access these thoughts, beliefs and emotions on a vibrational, energetic level. The sound waves, or frequencies, change the energetic structure of your energetic body where your thoughts and beliefs are stored. These stored aspects of your consciousness cannot be removed or destroyed, as one of the universal laws of nature is that energy cannot be created, nor destroyed, only transmuted into another vibration. The process of sound healing allows you to transmute and reprogram your aspects of consciousness into another, possibly healthier vibrational state. Therefore, sound healing is such an important tool for healing. It works on an energetic level that goes beyond the conscious mind.

As discussed earlier in the chapter of mindset, our thoughts and intent interact with the unseen world of energy in our universe, giving us the power to create our reality. When using sound and the voice for healing and shifting consciousness, it is important that the correct intention be used. This means that the thoughts in your mind, along with the emotional state that you are in before and during the creation of sound frequencies will encode those sound waves with the very energetic consciousness that you are thinking and feeling at the time. This means that it is particularly important when creating sounds for healing or shifting consciousness that your intent is focussed on what it is that you are wanting to achieve.

Think about one of your favourite musical artists or performers. What is it about them that you like? Apart from their personality, physical looks or moral views, what do you like about their performances? In music bands, the lead singer is usually the focus of the performance, literally the 'voice' of the band. Songs are usually based around concepts of emotional life experiences that the singer, or maybe someone else in the band has experienced. A good performance often leads people to say that they "put their whole heart into it". What you may not realise is that the singer, as well as the band members that play the instruments, are all energetically projecting their thoughts and emotions through the music. Their intent is projected on the sound waves of the musical sound vibrations being created. When you feel an emotion from listening to the music, you are not only being moved consciously by the musical melodies but also by the thoughts and emotional energy encoded on the sound waves. Even if it is a recording of a performance, the energy is still there, encoded in the sound waves.

Every human being can use sounds for healing. It is as natural an ability to us as is breathing the air around us. It is a common misconception that you need musical knowledge or ability to become a sound healer. This is not true. Unlike musicians, learning how to use sound for healing does not require knowledge of the musical scale, how to play an instrument, or even be a trained singer for that matter. Anyone can learn how to use sound for healing.

Sound healing covers many sound creation techniques such as using Tibetan singing bowls, chimes, tuning forks, drums and many more instruments for various cultures around the world. Probably the most versatile and simplest instrument that anyone can use is their own voice. Our voice is potentially the most powerful, convenient and effective of all sonic instruments available to us. We already have it within us. It does not need to be bought, stored anywhere, dusted regularly, cleaned etc. When used for healing, the voice is used to tone sounds that interact with our being. A common technique is to tone the vowel sounds i.e. A, E, I, O, U. Here is an exercise to sense sound vibrations in the body.

Exercise

1. Find a time and place where you will not be disturbed or any other factor that may make you feel self-conscious about making sounds

2. Sit somewhere comfortably

3. Take note of your state of mind and emotions. Let go of any thoughts or feelings that may be lingering from your day.

4. Set your intent on what it is that you want to achieve in this session. Although it may be a practise session, it is still important to focus your intent on what you want to achieve i.e., tone sounds better, heal an ache in your body, feel more peaceful etc.

5. Focus on your breath. Take a couple of deep breaths to move your awareness to your body and away from your mind

6. Tone an "AH" vowel sound, like the sound in the word, aha. Hold it as you completely breathe out the one breath

7. Take note of how it feels and where you might feel the vibration in your body.

Once you practice manipulating the mouth and tongue to make and hold the vowel sounds, more advanced techniques can be used to develop the harmonic, or overtone to these vowel sounds. Have you ever heard Tibetan monks or Mongolian throat singers? You might hear a whistling sound that seems to be a much higher pitch than the deep sound that they are also making. Those higher pitch sounds are called harmonics or overtones, which are a vibrational frequency much higher than the fundamental note. These overtones are usually much higher in frequency than what our voice can produce and are quite powerful when used with the right intent for healing.

So how does sound affect us? Sound interacts with us on many levels of our being. Remember that just like our eyes can see only a relatively small portion of the electromagnetic spectrum of energy as visible light, our sense of hearing can perceive only a small portion of the sound frequencies that are around us. Sounds that we cannot hear still affect our body, just as other forms of electromagnetic vibrational energy that we cannot see with our eyes can also affect our body, for example ultraviolet radiation from the sun that causes sun burn to the skin.

A good visual example of how sound waves can affect matter is a vibrational phenomenon called cymatics, based on a Greek word meaning 'wave'. Basically, this involves a process of generating sound waves via a speaker that is attached to a flat surface or bowl, creating shapes in powders, granular particles, pastes or liquids. The results are astounding, as specific sound frequencies create certain shapes in the medium. The powders and particles tend to move and gather into rather ornate two-dimensional patterns and shapes, whereas the liquids create three-dimensional shapes that appear to defy gravity, jumping up out of their previously resting state.

Although this is a relatively basic example of how sound waves affect physical matter, nevertheless it demonstrates just how powerful sound waves are in travelling through in our world, constantly changing the structure of the matter in our universe. Remember that everything in our universe vibrates, so the sound is not only affecting physical objects in our visual world, but also the matter around us that we cannot see with our naked eye. After seeing how the cymatics experiments affected liquids in such a powerful way and knowing that our bodies comprise of over 70% water, imagine then how our physical bodies are affected by the waves and frequencies of sound in our lives. How are these sounds changing the structure of our bodies? What about Dr Masaru Emoto's research of our consciousness affecting the structure of water that we mentioned in an earlier chapter? If we go back to what we discussed earlier about how it is not just the sound frequency itself but the thoughts and emotions that are used when creating the sound that give that sound the power to manifest that consciousness, this demonstrates the true power of using sound for healing.

Using Sound as a Tool for Intuition Development

Sound frequencies can shift our energetic vibration and consciousness, allowing an understanding of an aspect of our being that may not have otherwise been accessible. It is through the process of shifting of consciousness that a connection to the higher self and intuitive voice can be attained. Specific vocal toning focused on the heart centre will help to encourage a strong connection to the heart, the centre for enlightened intuition. Try this exercise to tap into the heart centre. Use the "AH" toning exercise mention earlier, but this time focus your thoughts on your heart centre. As you create the sound, feel the sound vibration in your heart area. Imagine that as you breathe, your breath is flowing in and out through your heart centre rather than through your mouth or nose. Keep focused on this technique for about five minutes, until it feels natural and you begin to feel the energy flow through the heart centre. With practice, this exercise will reconnect you to your heart, helping to enhance the voice of intuition.

My Journey with Sound

Anyone can learn how to use their voice and other sonic tools for healing and raising their consciousness. My journey began many years ago when I felt the need to explore meditation states to learn more about myself and my life. On what I would now say was a rather profound moment in my life, I remember being given a relaxation audio CD that comprised of vocal toning, mantras, Tibetan bowls, tuning forks and other sonic tools. The CD was called *Chakra Chants* by Jonathan Goldman, a pioneer in the field of sound healing based in the USA; someone who would inspire me for many years to come. After listening to those seven chakra tracks, I flowed into a state of total bliss. I was still conscious, yet my consciousness had risen to such a level that I had never experienced before. I saw life differently and sensed there was much more to learn. I wanted to learn more about this man and how those sounds were created. That moment initiated a whole new way of life for me. I left my old life and way of thinking behind, embarking upon a journey of self-exploration, as well as an exploration of sound healing, shifting consciousness and wanting to understand my life and ultimately, my purpose.

I began studying sound healing from many sources around the world, learning how to create and replicate those amazingly powerful healing sounds that I had heard on the CD. Through passionate self-teaching, as well as correspondence courses with Jonathan Goldman's teachers in the USA, I learned how to create those sounds. The profound realisation for me was understanding how sound can heal the body. During this journey I realised how powerful our consciousness is and what we 'vibrate to' consciously, we receive back in our lives.

Another empowering aspect of sound healing I discovered is that how it can promote an enlightened state of consciousness, enabling us to make a connection with a higher consciousness, allowing us to tap into the flow of intuition. When I began using sound healing to assist the healing of clients, I could sense that I was finally on the right pathway to expressing my life purpose; to demonstrate and teach the power of sound for healing and reconnection to our intuition, our higher-self.

About the Author

Kim Sowter

Author, Entrepreneur, Medium, Clairvoyant

Kim is an author, entrepreneur, medium and clairvoyant.

She was born with the ability to see and sense spirits. She also has the natural ability to know past and future events, as well as the ability to read individuals. When Kim was enrolled by her mother in kung fu classes at age eight, her teacher recognised her abilities and began to teach her meditation and how to further open up her inner sight.

As an adult, Kim lived alone for a short time in a haunted home. She left the home after just two weeks because she experienced a range of intense physical phenomena. As a result of this experience, she pursued three years of development as a trance medium and clairvoyant with the Victorian Spiritualist Church.

After earning her diploma in Theatre, specialising in lighting design, Kim worked with the Victorian State Opera, the Australian Ballet, and the Melbourne Theatre Company. For a while, she operated her own business in theatre and television until the pull to offer readings led her to work part time as a professional clairvoyant. Her clients included solicitors, celebrities and those who had lost loved ones. Ultimately, her interest in alternative health caused her to leave theatre and television and begin studying remedial massage and physiology. She went on to study medical intuition.

After her studies, she began working a 'regular' 9 to 5 job. This job gave her insight into how the average person lives. It also showed her the reasons why people get depressed, feel anxious, and lack motivation. This experience motivated her to apply her abilities to help people find their intuitive voice.

Kim's professional associations include the International Psychics Association and the International Institute of Complementary Therapists.

She has travelled and worked throughout Australia, Austria, Italy, the United Kingdom, North America, China, Thailand, Singapore, Malaysia and Germany.

Kim Sowter is co-author of *The Sentient Pathway* and lives in Victoria, Melbourne with her husband Ben.

About the Author

Ben Sowter

Author, Psychic, Medium, Sound Healer & Medical Intuitive

Ben is an author, psychic, medium, Sound Healer and medical intuitive.

Born in the working-class town of Newcastle, NSW, Ben, from a young age, typically loved to tinker with all things mechanical, pulling them apart to see how they worked. His technical creative ability led to pursuing a trade qualification as a fitter and turner. Leaving school at 16, Ben began an eight-year journey which led to various jobs and a romantic engagement.

Life never works out as you plan. In his mid-twenties, Ben had left home, worked for various companies, and been romantically engaged; but something was missing in life. It was time to leave the life he had been born into and to find the missing piece of the puzzle that seemed to be calling from deep within.

A move to a new state resulted in meeting a diverse range of cultures and beliefs. Ben later discovered that the inner yearning to 'find himself' had been his own intuition guiding him to a new and more wholesome way of living. This insight, along with his natural interest in learning what makes all things tick, opened the doorway to developing a keen interest in working out what causes human beings to be the way they are and how we can change our lives by following the inner voice.

Now, Ben works with various modalities that he uses as tools to assist with the inner process of connecting to ourselves on a deeper consciousness. His pursuits have allowed Ben to demonstrate his abilities within various Spiritual Churches, public speaking engagements about the power of sound and connection to our spiritual selves, workshops, and classes with various students all over the world.

He has travelled and worked throughout Australia, Thailand, Malaysia, Italy, Austria, Germany and the United Kingdom.

Ben's professional associations include the International Institute of Complementary Therapists, the International Psychics Association, the Sound Healers Association, and the Australian Medical Intuitives Association. Ben is also a qualified astrologer with the Victorian Astrologers Association.

Ben Sowter is co-author of *The Sentient Pathway* and lives in Victoria, Australia with his wife Kim.

RECOMMENDED RESOURCES